Feast with

MIDDLE EASTERN & MEDITERRANEAN FOOD

TAL SMITH

Photography by Russell Smith

JACANA

Following the positive response that we received from our first *Sababa* cookbook and the constant requests for more recipes, I thought it was time to write a second book. I have continued to keep the recipes simple, and hope that by sharing more recipes with you, you will continue to be encouraged to cook more home meals.

Easily accessible ingredients for my dishes are essential and you can find most of them on the shelves of almost any supermarket.

There is still a very strong family influence in all the recipes as this will always be the basis for my cooking. Family meals and celebrations form part of my strong Jewish and middle-eastern culture.

Working with my talented husband, Russell, is once again a privilege and a pleasure. I hope you enjoy his beautifully captured still-life photographs, making this new book incredibly beautiful.

For our beautiful Dans

CONTENTS

INTRODUCTION

SABABA TECHNIQUES AND PANTRY STAPLES

Garlic

In general I use a lot of garlic and refer to it as 'crushed garlic' in my recipes, but that doesn't mean the ready-made crushed garlic available at supermarkets – it means fresh garlic. I crush my own garlic and refrigerate it in batches, and when cooking use one teaspoon from this homemade supply. If you also cook regularly, this is worth doing to streamline the process. Break apart a head of garlic, peel the cloves and add to a food processor with just enough oil to moisten it and help it break down. It doesn't have to be extra-virgin olive oil – canola or sunflower is fine. Two to three heads of garlic will make about 250 ml and it will last for two to three weeks. But if you only cook once in a while, it is best to crush the garlic just before using. When shopping for fresh garlic, always look for really small, firm cloves.

Chilli

I also keep a little container of freshly ground chilli in the fridge, which I use in the same way as the garlic. You can also add one whole chilli (seeded and chopped) as included in the recipes, but what I really like to do is substitute my chilli sauce (see Zough on page 30). The sauce contains other ingredients like onion, garlic and spices, which add complexity to the final flavour.

Fried onion flakes

Fried onion flakes come up in quite a few Sababa recipes and I am often asked for details on where to find them. Atlas Trading in Cape Town sell one-kilogram bags, which is preferable to the small sachets sold in the salad section at supermarkets because I add them by the cup rather than by the tablespoon – mostly in rice dishes.

Caramelised onions

Caramelised onions have to be one of my favourite things. I know people often think 'caramelised' means adding sugar, but what I mean by this term is cooking the onions for a long period of time so their natural sweetness is accentuated – without adding sugar.

Cooking pulses

It is worth repeating that at Sababa we cook beans and chickpeas from scratch – I find the tinned varieties have an acidic taste. Taking the time to soak dried pulses overnight before cooking them the following day just takes a bit of forward planning, that's all.

ROSH HASHANAH

Over Rosh Hashana, the Jewish New Year, it is traditional to cook with certain ingredients to ensure a healthy, happy year ahead. Customers often ask my advice on what to cook over festivals, especially over New Year, so I've included a number of recipes that use one or more of these ingredients.

Ingredients

Below is a list of ingredients enjoyed by Sephardic Jews over Rosh Hashanah. The Sephardic culture originates in North Africa and the Mediterranean, while Ashkenazi Jews have Eastern European heritage. My father is a Sephardi and we follow his traditions. The reason these particular foods are important is their Hebrew names relate to Hebrew words that convey our wishes for the coming year. Each one is blessed before eating, to reinforce the symbolism.

- Apples, dipped in honey, renew a good year.
- With leeks the blessing states our enemies shall be cut down.
- Spinach symbolises our enemies departing.
- For dates a blessing is said to bring an end to our enemies.
- With pumpkin the blessing removes all evil decrees.
- Sesame increases our merits.
- Pomegranate represents the hope that we will be filled with mitzvoth (good deeds), in the same way that a pomegranate is filled with seeds.
- A fish or sheep's head is blessed so we may be a head and not a tail.

MEZZE DISHES

AUBERGINES

Aubergines come up a lot in Sababa recipes, especially in this chapter, so here is a quick recap on how we treat them.

Roasting

Cut the aubergines into wedges, arrange in a colander and sprinkle with salt to draw out any bitterness. Leave for at least 10 minutes or overnight. Before using the aubergines, simply wipe off all the moisture with a clean tea towel. Arrange them on a baking sheet with about 2 cm between them, and brush both fleshy sides of each wedge with olive oil – I brush one side, turn that side flat onto the baking sheet and then brush the other side. Season the wedges with salt and pepper and roast at 180°C for about 30 minutes or until soft on the inside and nicely browned on the outside.

If you don't have time to braai your whole aubergines, you can roast them in an oven preheated to 180°C for 40 minutes to 1 hour. They are ready when they look as if they might explode and the flesh sinks in when pressed. Peel and drain as with the charred aubergines (see below).

Charring

Cook whole aubergines over an open flame and keep turning so they cook evenly. Once the outside is blackened all over and the inside is very soft, set aside to cool. Remove the charred skin and leave the flesh in a colander for at least one hour to drain any excess liquid.

There are so many different flavours that combine well with aubergine and these are just a few. All the dips that follow are best prepared well in advance and refrigerated for at least a day before serving to improve consistency and allow flavours to develop. The aubergines should be charred so they impart that distinctive smoky flavour – bear this in mind when having a braai and add a few to the grid. These dips can be served as part of a mezze platter or as accompaniments to meat or fish or used as spreads.

Aubergine and Baby Marrow Mezze

- 1 large aubergine
- 500 g large baby marrow
- 3 tbsp Greek yoghurt
- ½ tsp garlic, crushed
- 1 tbsp lemon juice
- 2 tbsp dill, chopped finely
- salt and freshly ground black pepper
- extra virgin olive oil and za'atar for garnish

Prepare the aubergine in either of the forms on page 18. Cook the baby marrows on an open flame until they are charred and soft. Remove the flesh of the baby marrow too, discarding the skins.

Chop the aubergines and baby marrow up and then mix together with the yoghurt, garlic, lemon juice, dill, salt and pepper. To serve, spoon the dip into a bowl, drizzle over some extra virgin olive oil and sprinkle with some za'atar.

Makes about 300 ml

Aubergine and Red Onion Mezze

- 500 g aubergines
- 40 g red onion, chopped
- 4 tbsp extra virgin olive oil
- salt and freshly ground black pepper
- lemon, zest and juice

Prepare the aubergines on the braai as described page 18. Chop them on a chopping board with a sharp knife until almost smooth. Mix all the ingredients together in a bowl and adjust the seasoning with salt and pepper if necessary.

Makes about 300 ml

Aubergine and Mixed Pepper Mezze

- 500 g aubergines
- 2 red peppers
- 2 yellow peppers
- 1 tsp garlic, crushed
- 3 tbsp canola oil
- salt and freshly ground black pepper

Prepare the aubergines on the braai as described on page 18. Cook the peppers on the braai, turning them occasionally until they are charred on the outside. Remove them from the braai and leave them to cool down and steam in a closed plastic packet. Once they are cool enough to handle, peel the skin off and remove the seeds from inside. Using a hand blender, blend the peppers and aubergine together just for a few seconds to help them break down. Then stir in the garlic, oil and seasoning.

Makes about 750 ml

Aubergine and Mayonnaise Mezze

- 500 g aubergines
- 1 tsp garlic, crushed
- 3 tbsp Hellmann's mayonnaise
- salt and freshly ground black pepper
- 1 tbsp Italian parsley, chopped
- extra virgin olive oil for garnish

Prepare the aubergines on the braai as described on page 18. Chop them up on a chopping board with a sharp knife until almost smooth. In a bowl mix them with the garlic, mayonnaise, salt and pepper. To serve add some freshly chopped parsley and a drizzle of olive oil.

Makes about 300 ml

Aubergine and Tomato Mezze

I've been making this dish since I started Sababa and it still sells extremely well. It is delicious on bread, as a side dish to lamb and with falafel in a pita.

- 800 g aubergines, cubed
- ¼ cup extra virgin olive oil
- ¼ cup canola oil
- salt and freshly ground black pepper

SAUCE
- 1 onion, chopped
- 2 tbsp canola oil
- salt and freshly ground black pepper
- 1 tsp garlic, crushed
- 1 chilli, chopped
- 1 tsp paprika
- ½ tsp cinnamon
- ½ tsp cumin
- 100 g tomato paste
- 800 g tinned chopped tomatoes
- ½ cup water
- 2 tbsp sugar

Preheat the oven to 180°C. Mix the aubergines in a bowl with both the oils, salt and pepper. Roast them in the oven on a baking tray lined with baking paper, until golden and soft. This should take about 20-30 minutes.

In the meantime prepare the sauce in a saucepan. Fry the onions in the oil with salt and pepper until soft and translucent. Add the garlic and chilli and mix through. Add the spices and continue cooking for another minute. Mix in the tomato paste and let it cook for a few minutes. Add the tinned tomatoes and then the water and sugar. Reduce the heat and leave the sauce to cook for about 20 minutes.

Once the sauce is ready, and while it is still hot, mix it with the roasted aubergine cubes.

Makes about 1 litre

Aubergine Rolls with Ricotta and Herb Filling

- 200 g ricotta
- 100 g Danish feta
- 3 tbsp Italian parsley, chopped
- salt and freshly ground black pepper
- 600 g aubergines
- extra virgin olive oil
- lemon

Cook's Note

Slice the aubergines really thin and use a brush to apply the oil so the slices don't become too oily on roasting. For a smokier flavour, cook them on a griddle pan – it will just take a little longer.

Preheat the oven to 180°C. Prepare the filling by mashing the ricotta, feta, parsley and a pinch of black pepper together with a fork. Keep aside in the fridge.

Slice the aubergines lengthways so that they are 2–3 mm thick. Place the aubergine slices on a baking tray lined with baking paper. You may have to do this in batches or use a few baking trays. Brush them with olive oil and sprinkle a little salt and pepper onto each one. Roast the aubergine slices in the oven for about 10 minutes or until they are golden and soft.

Once the roasted aubergines have cooled down, lay them all side by side on a work surface. Add a teaspoon of the filling onto the bottom of each slice and roll them up tightly.

Squeeze some fresh lemon juice over them before serving.

Makes about 30

DIPS & SAUCES

Avocado and Chilli Dip

I often make this for dinner parties as a snack to serve on arrival. It is very citrusy and spicy, which I love, but you can tone it down if you prefer.

- 2 medium avocados
- 1 lemon, zest and juice
- ½ tsp chilli sauce OR 1 fresh chilli, chopped finely
- 10 g Italian parsley, chopped
- 10 g mint, chopped
- salt and freshly ground black pepper
- 2 tbsp extra virgin olive oil
- 1 tsp za'atar

Peel the avocados and mash them with a fork. In a bowl mix the avocados with the lemon zest and juice, fresh chilli or chilli sauce, chopped herbs, salt, pepper and 1 tbsp of the olive oil. Serve the dip in a bowl and garnish with 1 tbsp of olive oil and the za'atar.

Makes 300 ml

Zough (Chilli Sauce)

This is traditionally part of a mezze platter but, as mentioned earlier, chilli sauce can be more than a condiment. Keep it in the fridge and add a teaspoon to whatever you're cooking instead of using a whole chilli.

- 50 g red chillies, roughly chopped
- 50 g green chillies, roughly chopped
- 100 ml canola oil
- ¼ medium red onion, chopped
- 2 cloves garlic
- 2 ml paprika
- 4 ml salt
- 2 ml cumin, ground
- 1 ml black pepper, ground
- 30 g coriander, ground

Using a hand blender or food processor blend all the ingredients together until a smooth paste is formed. Adjust the seasoning with salt and pepper if necessary and add a little water or oil if it's too thick. Keep in the fridge.

Makes about 300 ml

Labneh

Labneh is an Arab cheese made by straining yoghurt to remove excess whey. We use labneh in many of our salads and as a spread for wraps. It is so easy to make and definitely worth a try.

- 1 kg natural yoghurt
- 1 tsp salt
- muslin cheesecloth and string

GARNISH
- 50 g Kalamata olives, chopped
- 10 g Italian parsley, chopped
- 20 g pine nuts, toasted
- 1 chilli, chopped (optional)
- 1 lemon, zest only
- ½ tsp garlic, crushed
- 20 g red onion, chopped finely
- ½ tsp sumac
- ½ tsp za'atar
- ¼ cup extra virgin olive oil

Mix the yoghurt with the salt. Place the muslin over a large bowl and pour in the yoghurt. Bring the sides of the cloth together and tie well. Tie the cloth over a kitchen sink and leave for about 24 hours, allowing all the liquid to strain off.

The yoghurt should now be thick and resemble a spread. Leave it in the fridge until you are ready to serve it.

For the garnish combine the rest of the ingredients together. When serving, spread the labneh in a bowl and top with the garnish. Serve with some warm pita breads.

Makes about 1 litre

Cook's Note
Depending on what flavour you're aiming for, you could use full-fat cow's milk yoghurt, goat's milk yoghurt or a combination of the two.

PICKLES

Pickled Cucumbers

This recipe comes from my maternal grandfather and it is one of the standard pickles that arrives with food in restaurants across Israel.

- 600 g Israeli cucumbers
- 10 g dill
- 4 bay leaves
- 4 cloves garlic, halved
- 1 tbsp whole peppercorns
- 5 cups water
- 2 cups spirit vinegar
- 4 tbsp salt
- 3 tbsp sugar

Sterilise a 2-litre jar by washing it with boiling water and leaving it to dry naturally. Wash the cucumbers and place them into the jar with the dill, bay leaves, garlic and peppercorns.

Boil the water, vinegar, salt and sugar together until the salt and sugar has dissolved. Pour the liquid into the jar and seal the lid tightly. Leave the cucumbers to pickle for 2 weeks in the fridge before eating.

Makes a 2-litre jar

Cook's Note
To ensure the pickled cucumbers remain crisp and retain their bright green colour, refrigerate as soon as the pickling liquid has been poured over and the jar is sealed.

Pickled Beetroot and Turnips

Beetroot is what gives pickled turnips their rosy pink colour – it looks more attractive and brightens up any table. Besides adding colour, pickles work particularly well with mezze.

- 700 g turnips, peeled and sliced
- 700 g beetroot, peeled and sliced
- 2 tbsp sugar
- 1 litre spirit vinegar
- 500 ml water
- 1 tsp salt

Fill a sterilised 2-litre jar with the sliced turnips and then the beetroots. In a pot, bring the rest of the ingredients to the boil and pour over the vegetables. Seal the jar and allow it to pickle for 5 days in the fridge.

Makes a 2-litre jar

MEZZE-STYLE SALADS

Tabbouleh

You can never add too much parsley to this salad – parsley and lemon just make it.

- 2 cups bulgur wheat
- 4 cups water
- 1 large English cucumber
- 400 g rosa tomatoes
- 3 lemons, juice and zest
- 60 g Italian parsley, chopped
- 100 ml extra virgin olive oil
- salt and freshly ground black pepper

Cook the bulghar wheat in boiling water for about 10 minutes or until it is soft and fluffy. Strain off all the liquid and leave to cool. In the meantime chop the cucumbers and tomatoes. Combine all the ingredients together, setting aside 5 tbsp of chopped parsley and the lemon zest.

Plate the salad and top off with the extra parsley and lemon zest.

Serves 10-12

Fattoush

The quality of this salad depends entirely on the quality of the ingredients.
It is basically an Israeli salad tossed with toasted pita, which is a great way
of using stale bread.

- 2 Turkish flatbreads/pita breads
- ¼ cup extra virgin olive oil
- 3 tsp za'atar
- 400 g Israeli cucumber, cubed
- 300 g rosa tomatoes, cubed
- 100 g radish, sliced
- 40 g red onion, chopped
- 10 g Italian parsley, chopped
- 10 g mint, chopped
- 1 tsp sumac
- 1 lemon, juiced
- salt and freshly ground black pepper

Preheat the oven to 180°C. Roughly tear the flatbreads and mix them in a bowl with 2 tbsp of olive oil and 2 tsp of za'atar. Toast them in the oven on a baking tray for about 10 minutes or until golden and crisp.

In the meantime combine the cucumbers, tomatoes, radish, red onion, herbs, sumac, lemon juice, and salt and pepper in a bowl. When you are ready to serve the salad, add the remainder of the olive oil, za'atar and toasted flatbread. Toss all the ingredients together and serve.

Serves 4–6

Cook's Note
I use small Israeli cucumbers, which have fewer seeds and are therefore less watery. You could add chopped Romaine lettuce for bulk or texture.

FRITTERS

Butternut and Leek Fritters

Both pumpkin and leek are traditional Rosh Hashanah ingredients so I've combined them, but you could make it with either one or the other. The leeks lend a silky sweetness and the butternut a smooth creaminess. For canapé parties I often serve these with some spiced labneh, but you could simply dust them with cinnamon-sugar.

- 500 g butternut, peeled and cubed
- 150 g leeks, chopped
- canola oil for frying
- salt and freshly ground black pepper
- ¾ cup flour
- 2 tsp baking powder
- ½ tsp cinnamon
- 2 tsp sugar
- 4 eggs

DUSTING
- 4 tbsp castor sugar
- ½ tsp cinnamon

Boil the butternut in water for about 15 minutes or until soft. Strain the water off through a colander and leave it to cool. In the meantime, fry the leeks in the oil with a pinch of salt and pepper.

Mash the butternut with a fork and then mix in the flour, baking powder, cinnamon, sugar and eggs.

Heat a non-stick frying pan with a little oil. Place a tablespoon of the batter into the pan. Once bubbles have formed and the bottom surface is golden and firm, flip the fritter over and continue cooking. Remove the fritters from the pan and place onto paper towel. Check the seasoning and adjust if needed. Otherwise repeat this process until all the mixture has been used up.

Prepare the dusting by mixing the castor sugar and cinnamon together. Serve the fritters warm or at room temperature with a dusting of the cinnamon-sugar.

Makes about 20

Spinach Fritters

This is something we serve over Rosh Hashanah, but it is lovely as a canapé any time of year.

- 2 onions, sliced
- canola oil for frying
- salt and freshly ground black pepper
- 1 kg Swiss chard
- 4 eggs
- ¾ cup flour
- 2 tsp baking powder
- 100 g ricotta
- 100 g Danish feta

Cook's Note
This recipe also works without the cheeses.

Start by frying the onions in 2 tbsp oil with some salt and pepper until soft and caramel brown.

Wash the Swiss chard well and then cook it with 2 tbsp oil in a pot until it wilts. Leave it to cool down in a colander and then squeeze out any excess liquid. Chop it up finely and then combine it with the onions, eggs, flour, baking powder and cheeses. Adjust the seasoning with salt and pepper if necessary.

Heat a non-stick frying pan with a little oil. Place 1 tbsp of the mixture into the pan. Leave it to cook for a minute until slightly golden and firm, flip the fritter over and continue cooking on the other side. Remove the fritter from the pan and place it on paper towel.

It is always a good idea to fry one fritter first and check the seasoning before frying the whole batch. If you are happy with the flavour, continue cooking the fritters until all the mixture has been used up.

Makes about 30

SOUPS

Broccoli and Baby Marrow Soup

This clean, healthy soup may sound dull, but it is surprisingly satisfying!

- 2 heads of broccoli, cut into florets
- 250 g baby marrow, cut into chunks
- 1 onion, cut into chunks
- 2 stalks celery, chopped
- 2 tbsp vegetable stock
- 800 ml water
- salt and freshly ground black pepper

Place all the ingredients together in a pot. Bring the liquid up to the boil and then continue cooking on a medium heat for about 30 minutes. Blend the soup with a hand blender and adjust the seasoning if necessary.

This soup can be served hot or cold with a dollop of crème fraîche.

Makes about 2 litres

Lentil and Vegetable Soup

Here the split lentils break down completely, creating a thick, creamy purée even though no cream is added.

- 1 onion, chopped
- 3 tbsp canola oil
- salt and freshly ground black pepper
- 100 g carrots, chopped
- 100 g celery, chopped
- 3 tbsp vegetable stock powder
- 150 g baby marrow, cubed
- 2 cups split lentils
- 2 litres water

Fry the onion in oil with a pinch of salt and pepper until soft and translucent. Add the carrot and celery and continue cooking for a few minutes. Mix through the stock and the rest of the ingredients. Bring the liquid up to the boil and then lower the heat. Cook the soup for about 40 minutes, stirring occasionally until the lentils have cooked through and dissolved into the soup.

Makes about 3 litres

Cook's Note
Try garnishing this soup with chopped parsley and toasted almonds and serve with toasted bruschetta.

Sweet Potato and Leek Soup

- 2 bunches leeks
- 2 tbsp canola oil
- salt and freshly ground black pepper
- 30 g celery leaves, chopped
- 500 g sweet potato, peeled and cubed
- 1 tbsp vegetable stock powder
- water

Clean the leeks well and chop. Heat the oil in a pot and fry the leeks with salt and pepper until soft. Add the celery leaves and cook until soft. Then add the sweet potato, stock and water. Bring the liquid to the boil and then simmer for about 40 minutes. Blend the soup with a hand blender, adding more water if it's too thick. Adjust the seasoning with salt and pepper if necessary.

Makes about 2 litres

Cook's Note
Leeks are more delicate than onions, and the flavour is concentrated in the bulb and pale stem. Use as much of the leek as possible and wash well as they are often sandy. Cut off the leafy top and discard. Slice down vertically from the leaf end, leaving the base of the bulb intact. Fan it open and rinse under cold water. As an extra precaution, soak in a bowl of cold water for a few minutes to allow any sand to sink to the bottom.

Mixed Bean Soup with Angel Hair Pasta

- 200 g dried chickpeas
- 200 g dried red kidney beans
- 200 g dried haricot beans
- 3 tbsp vegetable oil
- 2 onions, chopped
- salt and freshly ground black pepper
- 200 g carrots, grated
- 100 g celery leaves, chopped
- 2 tsp turmeric
- 1 tsp cayenne pepper
- 100 g tomato paste
- 400 g tinned diced tomatoes
- 2 tbsp vegetable stock powder
- 2 litres water
- 2 tbsp sugar
- 250 g angel hair pasta
- 20 g coriander, leaves picked

Cook's Note
You can use any combination of beans or pulses, but use dried rather than tinned. The pasta can be omitted.

Soak the chickpeas, red kidney beans and haricot beans overnight in 3 times the amount of water and in 3 separate bowls. The following day, strain off the water and rinse.

Cook the beans and chickpeas together in a pot of water for about 15 minutes or until soft. Then in a large pot heat the oil and cook the onions with salt and pepper until soft and translucent. Add the carrots and celery and continue cooking for a few minutes, stirring occasionally. Add the spices and then the tomato paste. Then add the beans and chickpeas, chopped tomatoes, stock, water and sugar. Bring the liquid to the boil and then reduce the heat so that the soup cooks on a medium heat for about 40 minutes. Adjust the seasoning with salt, pepper and sugar if necessary.

Cook the pasta in boiling water for about 10 minutes or until al dente. Strain the hot water off and run the pasta under cold water.

When serving add a portion of the pasta to each bowl and then cover it with the mixed bean soup and garnish with fresh coriander.

Makes about 3 litres

Cauliflower and Cheddar Soup

I love this classical pairing of cauliflower and cheese and find it comforting in winter. Although dairy is added, this soup is not at all rich or heavy.

- 3 tbsp vegetable oil
- 2 onions, diced
- salt and freshly ground black pepper
- 2 carrots, grated
- 2 celery stalks, chopped
- 800 g cauliflower, cut into florets
- 2 tbsp vegetable stock powder
- 1 litre water
- 200 g mature cheddar, grated
- 1 tsp English mustard
- 50 g Parmesan, grated

Heat the oil in a pot and fry the onions with salt and pepper until soft and translucent. Add the carrots and celery, and continue cooking for a few minutes. Stir in the cauliflower, stock and water. Bring the liquid to the boil and then reduce the heat so that the soup cooks gently for about 30 minutes.

Remove the pot from the heat and blend the soup with the cheddar and mustard until smooth. If you find the soup is too thick, then add more water. Adjust the seasoning with salt and pepper if necessary. For serving, add a couple of tablespoons of grated Parmesan to each bowl.

Makes about 2 litres

Safta's Cabbage Soup

This is from my maternal grandmother, Golda, and she and my grandfather would eat it all year round. I can still picture them sitting in their freezing-cold air-conditioned apartment in summer, eating their soup together over lunchtime.

- 1 tin sauerkraut (400 g)
- 100 g tomato paste
- 2 tbsp vegetable stock
- 2 tbsp sugar
- 1 ½ litres water
- salt and freshly ground black pepper
- 20 g butter
- 20 g flour

Drain the liquid from the sauerkraut. Place the sauerkraut, tomato paste, stock, sugar and water in a pot and bring to the boil. Lower the heat so that the liquid simmers and season with salt and pepper. Let the liquid simmer for about 40 minutes.

Melt the butter in the pan and then add the flour. Mix together well and continue cooking for about a minute. Add a ladle of the soup mix into the pan and mix together well so that the mixture is smooth and there are no lumps.

Add the mixture from the pan to the soup pot and cook together for a further 10 minutes until the soup has thickened.

Makes about 2 litres

Pumpkin and Ginger Soup

A great option for Rosh Hashanah if you're vegetarian or don't want to serve chicken soup. This soup is zesty and aromatic, thanks to plenty of ginger.

- 2 onions, chopped
- 3 tbsp canola oil
- salt and freshly ground black pepper
- 1 kg pumpkin, peeled and cut into chunks
- 100 g carrots, peeled and cut into chunks
- 500 g sweet potato, peeled and cut into chunks
- 80 g ginger, peeled
- 3 tbsp vegetable stock powder
- 1 litre water
- 20 g coriander, roughly chopped

Fry the onions in oil with a pinch of salt and pepper until soft and translucent. Add the pumpkin, carrots, sweet potato and ginger, and continue cooking for a few minutes. Mix through the stock and then add the water. Bring the liquid to the boil and then lower the heat.

Cook the soup on a medium heat for about 40 minutes, stirring occasionally. Blend until smooth using a hand blender and then check for seasoning, adding more salt and pepper if necessary. If you find the soup too thick, add more water. Garnish with fresh coriander before serving.

Makes about 3 litres

Brown Lentil Soup

This is my mom's recipe and, unlike split lentils, which are more common in soups, the brown lentils hold their shape.

- 2 onions, chopped
- 3 tbsp canola oil
- salt and freshly ground black pepper
- 150 g carrots, grated
- 150 g celery, chopped
- 2 tbsp vegetable stock powder
- 250 g small brown lentils
- 1 ⅕ litres water
- 30 g chopped parsley as garnish

Fry the onions in oil with a pinch of salt and pepper until soft and translucent. Add the carrot and celery, and continue cooking for a few minutes. Mix through the stock and lentils and then add the water. Bring the liquid up to the boil and then lower the heat. Cook the soup for about 40 minutes, stirring occasionally. Check the seasoning and add more salt and pepper if necessary. If you find the soup too thick, add more water.

Makes about 2 litres

FISH, MEAT & CHICKEN

Chraime Fishcakes

This recipe is heavily influenced by my Tripolitan (Libyan) heritage.
Chraime, which featured in our first book, is fillets of fish cooked in a red,
spicy sauce and it makes an appearance at most festivities. This is a variation
on that theme using fishcakes, and even my mom is a convert! Chraime just
isn't the same without some fresh white bread for mopping up the sauce or,
if it's a Friday night, some challah.

- 1 onion, diced
- 1 carrot, grated
- canola oil
- salt and freshly ground
  black pepper
- 500 g hake, filleted
- 20 g Italian parsley,
  chopped
- 20 g dill, chopped
- 1 egg

SAUCE
- 1 onion, diced
- salt and freshly ground
  black pepper
- 2 tbsp canola oil
- 6 tsp garlic, crushed
- 100 g tomato paste
- 2 cups water

For the fishcakes, fry the onion and carrot with 3
tbsp canola oil, salt and pepper until soft. Leave
this to cool. In the meantime mince the hake in a
food processor. In a bowl, combine the hake with
the herbs, egg and fried onion and carrot. Set
this mixture aside in the fridge while you make the
sauce.

Prepare the sauce by cooking the onion with salt
and pepper in the oil until soft and translucent.
Mix through the garlic and then add the tomato
paste. Cook for about a minute and then add the
water. Simmer the sauce for about 15 minutes.

In the meantime, fry the fishcakes in batches in a
non-stick pan with a little oil each time. Once all
the fishcakes are cooked through, add them to the
sauce and continue cooking a few more minutes.

Serves 6 – 8

Cajun Grilled Yellowtail

- 1 kg yellowtail, filleted
- 2 tbsp extra virgin olive oil
- 1 lemon, zest and juice
- 1 tbsp soy sauce
- ¼ tsp paprika
- ¼ tsp cumin
- ¼ tsp dried oregano
- ¼ tsp chilli powder
- ¼ tsp coriander, ground
- 10 g dill, finely chopped
- salt and freshly ground black pepper

Preheat the oven to 200°C. Marinate the fish in a bowl with all the ingredients for at least 30 minutes, making sure you rub the spices onto the fish well. Grill the fish on a baking tray for about 15 minutes or until it is firm to the touch.

Serves 4-5

Cook's Note
I love cooking yellowtail on the braai – just secure it in a fish grid and cook for 10 minutes per side over medium-hot coals. This marinade can be used for any linefish.

Lamb Meatballs

These are great with orzo (pasta rice) and I often warm up any leftover meatballs to have with a crisp wholewheat wrap, some grilled aubergine and hummus.

- 500 g lamb mince
- ½ onion, diced
- 2 eggs
- 10 g dill, chopped
- 10 g coriander, chopped
- 10 g mint, chopped
- 1 slice bread
- salt and freshly ground black pepper

SAUCE
- 1 onion, diced
- 2 tbsp vegetable oil
- salt and freshly ground black pepper
- ½ tsp garlic, crushed
- 2 tsp paprika
- 1 tsp cumin
- 1 tsp turmeric
- ¼ tsp cinnamon
- ¼ tsp nutmeg
- 50 g tomato paste
- 400 g tinned chopped tomatoes
- 2 cups water
- 20 g Italian parsley, chopped

Mix the lamb mince with the onion, egg and herbs. Soak the bread in water and then add it to the lamb with salt and pepper. Set the lamb mixture aside in the fridge and prepare the sauce.

Fry the onions in oil with salt and pepper until soft and translucent. Mix through the garlic and then the spices. Add the tomato paste and cook the mixture for another minute. Add the chopped tomatoes, water and parsley. Simmer the sauce for about 20 minutes, adding more water if necessary.

Once the sauce is ready, roll small balls of the lamb mince mixture and poach them in the sauce. Once all the balls are in the sauce, continue cooking for a further 10–15 minutes or until the lamb has cooked through and is well coated with the sauce.

Serves 4–5

Cook's Note
If possible, get your lamb freshly minced at the butcher. Beef or chicken mince can be substituted.

Chicken Koftes

These koftes are lighter than the traditional Middle-Eastern version made
with lamb – and they make a delicious burger patty.

- 1 slice bread
- 500 g chicken mince
- ½ onion, chopped
- 30 g Italian parsley, chopped
- 20 g coriander, chopped
- 1 egg
- 1 chilli, chopped
- ½ tsp paprika
- ½ tsp cumin
- salt and freshly ground black pepper
- 1–2 tbsp canola oil for frying

Cook's Note
**The bread can be left out
or substituted with 125 ml
cooked rice or bulgur.**

Soak the bread in a little water and then break
it up into a bowl with all the rest of ingredients
except for the oil. Season the mixture with salt and
pepper and combine all the ingredients together
well.

In a non-stick frying pan, heat up 1–2 tbsp oil.
Add a heaped tablespoon of the mixture into the
frying pan. Flatten the mix slightly with a fork and
leave to cook until lightly golden in colour. Flip
the mix over and continue cooking until golden
and the mixture has cooked through completely.
Remove the kofte from the pan and place it on
clean paper towel, allowing any excess oil to
drain off. Continue this process until all the mixture
has been used up. Depending on the size of your
frying pan, you should be able to cook quite a
few koftes at a time.

Makes about 10

Lamb and Leek Stew

This is one dish I keep coming back to when having people over for dinner. I cook it on the hob, transfer it to a casserole dish, add some water and leave it in the oven. And as long as there is enough liquid so it doesn't dry while you're having drinks and snacks, it actually improves. I always serve it with Carrot and Onion Rice (page 174) and Moroccan Lentil Stew (page 125).

- 1 large bunch leeks, trimmed and washed well
- 2 kg lamb goulash
- 500 g baby rosa tomatoes
- 400 g tinned chopped tomatoes
- 1 litre water
- ½ tsp cayenne pepper
- 2 tbsp paprika
- ½ garlic bulb, peeled
- 2 tbsp salt
- ½ tsp black pepper, ground
- 2 tbsp sugar
- 120 g tomato paste
- 2 tbsp chicken stock powder

Chop the leeks and then place all the ingredients together in a large pot. Bring the liquid to the boil and then reduce the heat so that the lamb cooks on a low-medium heat for about 2 hours or until it is soft and falls apart easily. If you find there is too much liquid in the pot, take the lid off for the last 20–30 minutes to that the sauce can reduce. Check the seasoning and add more salt and pepper if necessary.

Serves 8–10

Roast Chicken with Paprika and Fried Onion Flakes

A great mid-week meal because everything – vegetables included – goes
into one roasting pan.

- 1 kg chicken breast
- 200 ml extra virgin olive oil
- 1 cup fried onion flakes
- 1 tbsp garlic, crushed
- 3 tbsp paprika
- 1 tsp chicken stock powder
- ½ tsp cayenne pepper
- salt and freshly ground black pepper
- 300 g sweet potato, sliced 4-cm thick
- 200 g carrots, peeled and cut into chunks
- 200 g baby marrow, cut into chunks
- 1 garlic bulb, halved

Preheat the oven to 180°C. Halve the chicken breasts lengthways and marinate them with 120 ml olive oil, fried onion flakes, crushed garlic, paprika, chicken stock, cayenne pepper, salt and pepper.

Prepare the vegetables and mix them with 80 ml of the olive oil, and salt and pepper. Spread them out onto a large baking dish so they are not overlapping, and roast them for 30 minutes. Then add the marinated chicken and any leftover marinade to the baking dish. Roast the chicken and vegetables together for about 20 minutes or until the chicken has cooked through.

Serves 5-6

Cook's Note
You can use chicken pieces instead – just add them with the vegetables and cook for 40 minutes in total.

Pepper Crusted Beef Fillet with Salsa Verde

Fillet continues to be popular at Sababa, probably because it is lean and tender and we have a health-conscious clientele. Personally I find fillet quite plain and love adding an accompaniment that is full of flavour, like salsa verde. This green, herby Italian sauce is traditionally made with anchovies but I haven't included them in this recipe.

- 1 kg beef fillet
- ¼ cup extra virgin olive oil
- 1 tbsp black pepper, crushed
- ½ tsp black pepper, fine
- 1 tsp garlic, crushed
- 1 tsp za'atar
- 2 tsp salt

SAUCE
- 30 g basil
- 30 g Italian parsley
- 2 cloves garlic
- 1 tbsp capers
- 3 cocktail gherkins, chopped
- 1 tsp hot English mustard
- 1 tbsp red wine vinegar
- ½ cup extra virgin olive oil
- salt and freshly ground black pepper

Marinate the fillet with all the ingredients except for the salt for at least an hour in the fridge.

In the meantime prepare the sauce by blending all the ingredients together with a hand blender until smooth. Set the sauce aside in the fridge until you are ready to serve the meat.

Preheat the oven to 200°C and bring the fillet to room temperature before roasting. Once the oven is hot, salt the fillet and roast for about 20 minutes. Allow the fillet to rest for at least 15 minutes before slicing, otherwise all the juice will run out and you will be left with dry beef.

Serve the fillet sliced with a large dollop of the herb sauce per serving.

Serves 5-6

Cook's Note
Chopping the herbs by hand will give a more textured (and authentic) salsa verde, and you could also prepare it using a pestle and mortar.

Chilli Chicken Curry

Serve with rice or couscous to soak up all the sauce in this warming curry.

- 1 kg chicken breast, cut into cubes
- 80 g ginger, grated
- 1 tsp garlic, crushed
- ½ cup yoghurt
- ¼ tsp nutmeg
- ½ tsp cumin
- ½ tsp garam masala
- salt and freshly ground black pepper

SAUCE
- 50 g ginger, grated
- 1 cup cream
- 1 tsp sugar
- 2 red chillies, chopped
- 1 tsp cumin
- 1 tsp paprika
- ½ tsp cayenne pepper
- 100 g tomato paste
- 2 cups water
- 1 lemon, juiced
- 30 g coriander, chopped
- 200 g salted butter
- salt and freshly ground black pepper

Marinate the chicken with the ginger, garlic, yoghurt, nutmeg, cumin and garam masala for an hour in the fridge.

Preheat the oven to 180°C and cook the chicken on a baking tray with salt and pepper for about 20 minutes.

In the meantime, prepare the sauce. Place the ginger, cream, sugar, chillies, spices, tomato paste and 2 cups of water into a saucepan and bring to the boil. Add the lemon juice and coriander and simmer for about 15 minutes. Melt the butter in a pan and then add it to the sauce. Adjust the seasoning with salt and pepper if necessary.

When the chicken is ready, add it to the saucepan with the sauce, mix through and serve.

Serves 6

Chicken and Date Casserole

This makes a great Rosh Hashanah main dish. Dates are highly nutritious and are bursting with sweetness, especially when cooked.

- 1 kg chicken breast, cut into strips
- 150 g dried, pitted dates
- 2 tsp paprika
- ½ cup red wine vinegar
- 1 cup extra virgin olive oil
- 1 tsp dried oregano
- 6 cloves garlic, halved
- 10 bay leaves
- ½ tsp crushed black pepper
- 1 tbsp sugar
- salt

Combine the chicken with all the ingredients except the salt, and leave it to marinate for at least 2 hours in the fridge.

Preheat the oven to 180°C. Add salt to the chicken. In a casserole dish, cook the chicken for about 20 minutes or until it has cooked through. Be careful not to overcook it so that it stays tender and soft.

Serves 5-6

Pan-fried Chicken and Onions

A perfect filling for pitas – just add some chopped salad and tahini and you have a complete meal. The onions make this dish, so don't be surprised by the quantity.

- 600 g chicken breast
- ¼ cup vegetable oil
- 3 onions, diced finely
- salt and freshly ground black pepper
- 1 tsp paprika
- 1 tsp cumin
- 1 tsp turmeric

Cut the chicken into strips. Heat the oil in a large frying pan and cook the onions with salt and pepper until soft and brown. Add the spices and cook them in the pan for about a minute. Add the chicken strips and cook for 10 minutes, mixing occasionally.

Serves 3–4

Chicken, Pea and Potato Stew

A classic from my childhood and a delicious one-pot meal.

- ¼ cup vegetable oil
- 2 onions, diced
- salt and freshly ground black pepper
- 1 tsp garlic, crushed
- 1 chilli, chopped
- 2 tsp turmeric
- 1 tsp paprika
- 3 cups frozen peas
- 1 kg chicken pieces, skinless thighs and drumsticks
- 500 ml water
- 30 g coriander, chopped
- 600 g potatoes, peeled

Heat the oil in a pot and fry the onions with salt and pepper until soft and translucent. Stir in the garlic and then add the chilli and spices. Add the peas, chicken pieces, water and coriander and cook for about 20 minutes on a medium heat. Cut the potatoes lengthways into slices 2–3 cm thick. Add the potatoes and more water if necessary and continue cooking for another 20 minutes or until the potatoes have cooked through.

Serves 5–6

Cook's Note
I love using chicken thighs and drumsticks because the meat is tender and simply falls off the bone when cooked. If you use chicken breast fillets, just slice them into strips and add along with the potatoes to avoid them drying out. The potatoes are only added for the last 20 minutes of cooking so they hold their shape – be careful not to overcook them.

Chicken Kebabs

These are great served with the Couscous with Sumac and Tzatziki on page 114.

- ½ tsp turmeric
- 2 tsp paprika
- 1 tsp garlic, crushed
- ½ tsp chilli powder
- 30 g soft herbs (dill, coriander, Italian parsley)
- 80 ml olive oil
- 1 kg chicken thighs, skinned and deboned
- salt and freshly ground black pepper
- 14–18 skewers (15 cm long is perfect)

Using a hand blender, combine all the ingredients together except for the chicken and salt to form a smooth paste.

Rub the paste onto the chicken thighs. Skewer 2–3 thighs onto each skewer and leave to marinate for at least 2 hours in the fridge.

When you are ready to cook the kebabs, add the salt. These are great on the braai and should be cooked on a medium heat until the chicken has cooked through. This should take about 10 minutes on each side.

Serves 6–8

Cook's Note
Alternatively, char the kebabs on a griddle pan for 2 minutes per side and cook for about 15 minutes in an oven preheated to 180°C. Skinless, boneless chicken thighs make all the difference when making kebabs because they remain succulent and tender.

Preserved Lemon and Chilli Chicken

Try serving this with labneh and warm pita breads.

- 140 g preserved lemons (see below)
- 1 ⅕ kg chicken thighs (with skin and bone)
- 2 tsp chilli sauce
- 2 sprigs rosemary
- 4 sprigs thyme
- 3 tbsp extra virgin olive oil
- 1 tsp cumin
- 1 tsp paprika
- 1 lemon
- salt and freshly ground black pepper

Cut the flesh away from the preserved lemon and discard. Then slice up the skins. Combine the chicken with all the ingredients except the lemon and the salt, and leave it to marinate for at least 2 hours in the fridge. The best way to do this is to rub all the ingredients with your hands into the chicken.

Preheat the oven to 180°C. Cut the lemon in half and put the halves into a casserole dish with the chicken and any leftover marinade. Roast the chicken for about 40 minutes or until it has cooked through and the skin is crispy.

Serves 4-6

Cook's Note
Although our customers often prefer chicken breasts, I find thighs are the tastiest part of the chicken. If you can find skinless, boneless thighs, these will also work well. If you prefer chicken breast fillets, just halve them lengthways and cook at about 180–190°C for 15 minutes.

Preserved Lemons

Preserved lemons can transform a dish from good to amazing. They need to be made at least two weeks in advance, so it is worth making a couple of jars when lemons are in season.

- 8 lemons, unwaxed
- 8 tbsp coarse salt
- 2 red chillies
- 3 rosemary sprigs
- 8 lemons, juiced
- extra virgin olive oil

Sterilise a 1-litre jar by washing it with boiling water and leaving it to dry naturally. Wash the lemons well and then cut a deep cross all the way from the top, but leaving the base intact. You should basically be left with 4 quarters attached. Add a spoonful of the salt inside each lemon and fill the jar with these stuffed lemons, chilli and rosemary. Push the lemons down into the jar and seal with a lid. Leave the jar in the fridge for a week and then add the lemon juice and olive oil. Seal the jar again and leave it for 4 weeks in a cool place. They will then be ready for use, but the longer they are left, the better they become.

Makes a 1-litre jar

Roast Leg of Lamb

The lamb will need some time to marinate, but once it is in the oven you can forget about it for a few hours. The meat should fall apart when pulled and can be shredded for stuffing into a pita with a crunchy salad and some of our dips.

- 1 lemon
- 1 kg deboned leg of lamb
- 4 cloves garlic, halved
- 8 small sprigs rosemary
- 80 ml extra virgin olive oil
- ½ tsp crushed black pepper
- ½ tsp paprika
- ½ tsp cumin, ground
- ½ tsp coriander seeds
- 1 onion, quartered
- 1 tbsp chicken stock powder
- 500 ml water
- salt

Start by removing the zest from the lemon and setting it aside. Cut the lemon into quarters.

Pierce the lamb in 8 different spots with a sharp knife and then insert half a garlic clove and a sprig of rosemary into each piercing. Rub the lamb with the olive oil, lemon zest, black pepper, paprika, cumin and coriander. Leave to marinate for a few hours or overnight.

When you are ready to cook the lamb, put it in a casserole dish with the lemon and onion quarters. Mix the stock powder with 500 ml boiling water and pour it into the casserole dish. Salt the lamb and cover the dish with foil. Roast at 180°C for 1 hour.

Remove the foil and continue to roast in the oven for a further 30–45 minutes or until the lamb is browned and tender, making sure there is always liquid in the dish. Once the lamb is ready, squeeze the juice from the lemons onto the lamb. Leave it to cool and then slice or shred the lamb. Before serving, pour over all the leftover juices from the roasting pan.

Serves 5-6

SALADS & VEGETARIAN DISHES

Sweet Potato Mash

Sweet potatoes are my new favourite ingredient (I love them almost as much as I love aubergines!) and this is a very more-ish recipe.

- 2 onions, sliced thinly
- 2 tbsp canola oil
- salt and freshly ground black pepper
- 2 kg sweet potatoes, peeled and cubed
- 120 g salted butter
- 1 cup cream
- 1 tbsp salt

Cook's Note
This is just as good made with regular potatoes.

Fry the onions in oil with a pinch of salt and freshly ground black pepper until soft and golden brown.

Boil sweet potatoes in a pot of boiling water for about 15–20 minutes or until soft. Strain the water off through a colander and leave for a few minutes, allowing all the liquid to strain off. Mash the sweet potatoes in a bowl while still hot, and mix in the butter until it has melted through. Heat the cream up in a saucepan and then pour it over the mashed potato mix. Mix the cream through and add salt to taste.

Mix half of the fried onions into the mash. Use the rest of the fried onions for garnish when serving.

Serves 10–12

Mushroom and Tahina Salad with Peas

A new Sababa recipe, which has just taken off – our customers can't seem to get enough of it! Since publishing our first cookbook, people are far more open to using tahini and we are selling so much more of it. This is just one example of tahina turning a few simple ingredients into something special.

- 2 cups frozen peas
- 200 g mushrooms, thinly sliced
- 150 g mangetout, finely chopped
- 20 g Italian parsley, chopped
- 20 g chives, chopped
- ¼ cup extra virgin olive oil
- salt and freshly ground black pepper

TAHINA
- 1 cup tahini paste
- 1 lemon, juiced
- 1 tsp crushed garlic
- ¾ cup water
- ½ tsp salt

Start with the dressing by mixing all the ingredients together with a whisk until smooth. Pour boiling water over the frozen peas and then strain the water off. Prepare all the vegetables and herbs and put them into a large bowl. Just before serving, add the tahina and olive oil to the vegetables and herbs. Season with salt and pepper.

Serves 8 – 10

Blanched Broccoli Salad with Mixed Sesame, Za'atar and Tahina

I like broccoli when it is bright green and still has some crunch, but it can be quite boring so the tahina makes it more interesting.

- 2 large heads of broccoli

TAHINA
- 1 cup tahini paste
- 1 lemon, juiced
- 1 tsp crushed garlic
- ¾ cup water
- ½ tsp salt
- ¼ cup extra virgin olive oil
- 1 tbsp za'atar
- 20 g black sesame seeds
- 20 g white sesame seeds

Bring a pot of water up to the boil. Place the whole broccoli one at a time into the boiling water. Leave for 30 seconds, turn over and leave for a further 30 seconds. Run the broccoli under cold water and then leave it to strain in a colander for at least 10 minutes so that all the water strains off.

In the meantime prepare the dressing by mixing the tahini paste, lemon juice, garlic, water and salt together until smooth. Keep the dressing in the fridge until you are ready to serve the salad.

Cut the broccoli into florets and mix them together with the olive oil, za'atar and half the black and white sesame seeds. Plate the broccoli onto a platter and just before serving, drizzle over the tahina and sprinkle the rest of the sesame seeds over the top.

If you find the tahina too thick, simply add more water and lemon juice.

Serves 6-8

Aubergine, Tahina and Roast Mushroom Salad

Another Sababa bestseller that could work as a stand-alone meal with some toasted pita breads on the side.

- 1 kg aubergines
- salt and freshly ground black pepper
- 500 g button mushrooms, quartered
- 1 red pepper, sliced
- 1 yellow pepper, sliced
- 1 red onion, sliced
- 2–3 sprigs oregano
- extra virgin olive oil
- 200 g fine green beans, cut in half

TAHINA
- ½ cup tahini paste
- 1 lemon, juiced
- ½ cup water
- ½ tsp garlic, crushed
- ¼ tsp salt

Preheat the oven to 180°C. Cut the aubergines into medium thickness wedges. Sprinkle salt over them and, after 10 minutes, wash and dry them. Put the aubergine wedges flat down onto the baking tray. Brush with olive oil and sprinkle with salt and black pepper. Roast the aubergines in the oven until they are soft and slightly crisp. Once they are ready, leave them to cool.

Mix the mushrooms, peppers, onion and oregano with 3 tbsp olive oil and salt and pepper. Roast them on a tray in the oven for about 20 minutes.

In the meantime bring a pot of water to the boil. Add the green beans and after a minute strain off the water and then run them under cold water. Leave them to dry and then mix them together with the rest of the roast vegetables.

Prepare the tahina by whisking all the ingredients together.

To assemble the salad, simply place the aubergine wedges on a platter, pour over the tahina and then top it off with the mixed roast vegetables.

Serves 8–10

Couscous with Sumac and Tzatziki

One of my most beautiful memories is visiting my safta's (grandmother's) house and watching her sit at her worktable and roll semolina to make couscous from scratch. Unfortunately our modern lifestyle doesn't allow for such time-consuming preparations and these days almost everyone buys it dried and packaged – except my safta, of course!

- 2 cups water
- 2 tbsp vegetable oil
- 1 tsp vegetable stock powder
- 2 tsp sumac
- 2 cups couscous
- 1 tsp cumin
- 2 lemons, zest and juice
- 30 g Italian parsley, chopped
- 60 g pecan nuts, toasted and chopped
- salt and freshly ground black pepper

TZATZIKI
- 200 g cucumber, grated
- 300 g yoghurt
- 1 tsp garlic, crushed
- 2 tbsp mint, chopped
- salt and freshly ground black pepper

Bring 2 cups of water to the oil, vegetable stock powder and sumac to the boil. Add the couscous and mix through until all the water has been absorbed. Place the lid onto the pot and leave the couscous to steam for about 5 minutes. Break the couscous up with a fork and then leave it to cool down.

Once the couscous is cool, add the cumin, lemon zest and juice, parsley and pecan nuts. Check for seasoning and add more salt and pepper if necessary.

For the tzatziki, simply combine all the ingredients together.

Serves 6-8

114

Cabbage Salad with Gherkins

This is my mom's *favourite* salad.

- 500 g green cabbage
- 300 g small cocktail gherkins
- 4 tbsp Hellmann's mayonnaise
- 40 g dill, chopped
- ½ cup canola oil
- 1 tsp sugar
- salt and freshly ground black pepper

Shred the cabbage very finely and chop the gherkins into small dice. Combine all of the ingredients together in a bowl and mix well. Check the seasoning and adjust if necessary.

Serves 8 – 10

Cook's Note
As with the cabbage salad in our first cookbook, take the time to shred the cabbage by hand.

Pickled Cabbage and Carrot Salad

Because of the lemon, this salad has an almost pickled flavour.

- 500 g green cabbage
- 300 g carrots
- 40 g dill, chopped
- ½ cup extra virgin olive oil
- 2 lemons, juiced
- 2 tbsp red wine vinegar
- 1 tsp sugar
- salt and freshly ground black pepper

Shred the cabbage very finely and chop the carrots into small dice. Combine the rest of the ingredients together in a bowl and mix well. Check the seasoning and adjust if necessary.

Serves 8 – 10

Cook's Note
**I chop the carrots by hand, but to save time and effort you could just grate them.
I also recommend that you shred the cabbage by hand.**

Cabbage Salad with Lentils, Cranberries and Goat's Cheese

A great combination of sweet and sour as well as being a substantial meal on its own.

- 120 g small brown lentils
- 100 g green cabbage
- 250 g red cabbage
- 1 cup cranberries
- 20 g Italian parsley, chopped finely
- 20 g wild rocket
- 1 lemon, zest and juice
- ½ cup extra virgin olive oil
- 50 g flaked almonds, toasted
- salt and freshly ground black pepper
- 100 g Chevin goat's cheese

Cook the lentils in boiling water for about 10 minutes or until they are just cooked. Be careful not to overcook them so they don't fall apart and have a grainy texture. Strain them through a colander and then wash under cold water so they cool down quickly.

Shred the cabbages very finely. Place them with the lentils, cranberries, parsley and rocket in a bowl. When you are ready to serve, add the lemon zest and juice, olive oil, half the flaked almonds and season with salt and pepper. Plate the salad in a bowl or platter and crumble over the goat's cheese. Sprinkle over the rest of the almonds and serve.

Serves 6-8

Cook's Note
Don't forget to shred the cabbage by hand!

Kale and Mixed Bean Salad

Kale is so popular at the moment I had to come up with a Sababa recipe!
This is healthy and hearty with a bit of sweetness from the fruit and some
crunch from the pecan nuts.

- ½ cup dried red kidney beans
- ½ cup dried haricot beans
- ½ cup dried small brown lentils
- 120 g kale
- ½ cup dried cranberries
- ½ cup dried mango, chopped
- ¼ cup extra virgin olive oil
- salt and freshly ground black pepper
- 50 g pecan nuts, toasted and chopped

Soak the beans separately overnight in 3 times the amount of water. The next day wash them and cook separately in boiling water until soft. Cook the lentils as well in boiling water. Once the beans and lentils have cooled down, mix in the rest of the ingredients except the pecan nuts. Add salt and pepper to taste. When you are ready to serve the salad, plate it and then sprinkle the pecans nuts over the top.

Serves 5-6

Cook's Note

Kale can be quite tough, so it is important to add the dressing – and the longer it marinates, the softer it becomes. Sometimes I dress the kale and leave it overnight, but if you like kale's natural texture, this is not necessary. I also chop the leaves really fine, treating them as I would herbs, because the smaller you chop them, the quicker they soften. When buying kale, always look for a deep green colour and a moist, hard stem.

Shakshuka with Aubergine

I make this version for my stand at the Oranjezicht City Farm Market every Saturday and it always sells out quickly!

- 1 onion, diced
- salt and freshly ground black pepper
- 4 tbsp vegetable oil
- 1 tsp garlic, crushed
- 1 red chilli, sliced (optional)
- 400 g aubergines, cubed
- 2 tbsp tomato paste
- 1 kg over-ripe plum tomatoes, chopped
- 1 tsp sugar
- 2 cups water
- 8 eggs
- 1 tsp cumin
- labneh for serving

In a large pan, fry the onion with salt and pepper in the oil until they are soft and translucent. Add the garlic and chilli and cook for a minute. Add the aubergines and cook until they are soft. Then add the tomato paste, tomatoes, sugar and water.

Cook for about 20 minutes on a low heat, allowing the sauce to reduce slightly and the flavours to develop. If you find the sauce is too thick, add more water. Crack the eggs into the pan and leave them to cook for about 10 minutes or until they are cooked to your liking. Sprinkle the yolks with cumin and serve each portion with a dollop of labneh and some basic white bread.

Serves 4

White Bean Stew

A satisfying vegetarian main that works brilliantly with plain couscous.

- 250 g dried haricot beans
- 2 onions, chopped
- 3 tbsp canola oil
- salt and freshly ground black pepper
- 1 tsp garlic, crushed
- 1 red chilli, chopped
- 60 g ginger, grated
- 2 tsp turmeric
- 2 tsp paprika
- 1 tsp cumin
- 2 cups frozen peas
- 40 g coriander, chopped
- 5 cups water
- 400 ml coconut milk

Soak the beans overnight in 3 times the amount of water. The next day, strain the water off and wash the beans. Cook them in boiling water for about 20 minutes until they are soft.

In a pot, fry the onions in the oil with salt and pepper until soft and translucent. Mix through the garlic, chilli and ginger, and then the spices. Add the beans, peas, coriander and about 5 cups of water. Bring the liquid up to the boil and then simmer for about 30 minutes, allowing all the flavours to develop and the liquid to reduce. Add the coconut milk and continue cooking for a further 10 minutes. Adjust the seasoning with salt and pepper if necessary.

Serves 6-8

Moroccan Lentil Stew

Serve as a vegetarian curry with rice or as a side to a meaty main course, like the Lamb and Leek Stew on page 76.

- 150 g dried small brown lentils
- 1 onion, diced
- 2 tbsp canola oil
- salt and freshly ground black pepper
- 1 tsp garlic, crushed
- 1 tbsp paprika
- 1 tbsp cumin
- 1 tbsp garam masala
- ½ tsp cinnamon
- ½ tsp cayenne pepper
- 1 tbsp tomato paste
- 1 cup tinned chopped tomatoes
- 150 ml water
- 1 tsp sugar

Cook the lentils in boiling water for about 10–15 minutes until they are soft. Strain the water off through a sieve.

Fry the onion in oil with a pinch of salt and pepper until soft and golden brown. Add the garlic and then the spices and mix through. Add the tomato paste and then mix through the chopped tomatoes, water and sugar. Add the cooked lentils and cook the stew for about 30 minutes, adding more water if necessary.

Check the seasoning and add more salt and pepper if necessary. Serve hot with some rice.

Serves 4–5

Cook's Note
You want the lentils to break down completely, so it is important to cook them properly before adding to the sauce.

Chickpea, Fennel and Tomato Stew

Some people are put off by fennel because they are concerned it might be overpowering, but here it really is quite subtle. Although this recipe involves some prep time for chopping all the vegetables, once it is on the hob you can just leave it to simmer. Serve with couscous, rice or even some toasted pita breads.

- 100 g dried chickpeas
- 1 onion, diced
- 2 tbsp canola oil
- salt and freshly ground black pepper
- 220 g fennel bulb, chopped
- ½ tsp garlic, crushed
- 1 red chilli, chopped
- ½ tsp turmeric
- 1 tsp paprika
- ¼ tsp cumin
- 7 ml vegetable stock powder
- 50 g tomato paste
- 30 g Italian parsley, chopped
- 4 cups water
- 1 potato, peeled and cubed
- 1 carrot, peeled and cubed
- 1 baby marrow, cubed
- 20 g Italian parsley, roughly chopped

Soak the chickpeas overnight in 3 times the amount of water. The next day, strain the water off and wash the chickpeas. Cook them in boiling water for about 20 minutes or until they are soft.

In a pot, fry the onions in the oil with salt and pepper until soft and translucent. Add the fennel and cook for a further minute. Mix through the garlic and chilli, and then the spices and stock powder. Add the tomato paste and mix through. Add the chickpeas, parsley and about 4 cups of water. Bring the liquid to the boil and then lower the heat so that the liquid simmers for about 30 minutes, allowing all the flavours to develop and the liquid to reduce. Add the potato, carrot and baby marrow and cook for a further 15 minutes or until the vegetables are soft but not falling apart. Adjust the seasoning with salt and pepper if necessary. Garnish with fresh Italian parsley.

Serves 6–8

Aubergine and Caramelised Onion Salad

The combination of aubergine, fried onions, flaked almonds and tahina is
hard to beat – just add flatbreads for a perfect starter.

- 1 kg aubergines
- extra virgin olive oil
- salt and freshly ground
  black pepper
- 1 onion, sliced
- 2 tbsp canola oil
- 20 g Italian parsley,
  chopped
- 30 g flaked almonds,
  toasted

DRESSING
- ¼ cup tahini paste
- 2 tbsp lemon juice
- ¼ cup water
- ¼ tsp salt
- ¼ tsp garlic, crushed
- 1 tbsp Italian parsley,
  chopped
- 2 tbsp natural yoghurt

Preheat the oven to 180°C. Cut the aubergines
into medium-thick wedges. Sprinkle salt over and
after 10 minutes, wash and dry them. Put them flat
down onto a baking tray and brush with olive oil
and sprinkle with salt and black pepper. Roast
the aubergines in the oven until they are soft and
slightly crisp. Once they are ready, leave them to
cool.

In the meantime, cook the onion in canola oil with
salt and pepper until soft and caramel brown in
colour.

Prepare the dressing by whisking all the
ingredients together, besides the parsley and
yoghurt. Once the dressing is smooth, mix in the
chopped parsley and yoghurt.

To assemble the salad simply layer the aubergine
wedges with the caramelised onions, parsley and
tahina-yoghurt dressing. Sprinkle over the toasted
almonds and serve.

Serves 4-6

Tomato and Creamy Feta Salad

I always make this salad at the shop when we are very busy and need to get something out fast.

- 500 g baby rosa tomatoes
- 2 bunches spring onions
- 20 g dill
- 20 g chives
- 200 g Danish feta
- ½ cup extra virgin olive oil
- salt and freshly ground black pepper

Cut the tomatoes in half and finely chop the spring onion, dill and chives. When you are ready to serve the salad, crumble over the feta, add the olive oil, and season with salt and pepper. Mix all together.

Serves 5-6

Cook's Note
Only mix the salad after adding the olive oil so it helps bind the ingredients. You don't want to over mix as the salad will turn mushy.

Cucumber, Lentil and Feta Salad

I love adding lentils to a salad, especially here, where they add an unexpected earthy flavour against the fresh, cooling cucumber.

- 500 g cucumber
- 250 g small brown lentils
- 250 g celery stalks, chopped
- 250 g Danish feta, crumbled
- ½ cup extra virgin olive oil
- 40 g Italian parsley, finely chopped
- 1 lemon, zest and juice
- salt and freshly ground black pepper
- 1 red chilli (optional)

Cut the cucumber in half lengthways and, using a teaspoon, scoop out all the seeds. Cut it into chunks. Cook the lentils in boiling water for about 15 minutes or until just soft. Strain the water off and leave them to cool down completely.

When you are ready to serve the salad, simply mix all the ingredients together well.

If you would like to serve this salad with chilli, chop it finely and then mix with a tablespoon of extra virgin olive oil and set aside.

Serves 8 – 10

Roast Cauliflower Salad with Green Beans and Tahina Dressing

- 700 g cauliflower
- 4 tbsp extra virgin olive oil
- 1 tsp turmeric
- 1 tsp paprika
- 1 tsp cumin
- ½ tsp cayenne pepper
- salt and freshly ground black pepper
- 200 g fine green beans, blanched
- ¼ red onion, sliced finely
- 60 g rocket

TAHINA
- ¼ cup tahini paste
- ¼ cup water
- 1 tbsp lemon juice
- ¼ tsp garlic, crushed
- 1 tbsp Italian parsley, chopped
- 1 tbsp dill, chopped

Start by making the tahina. Combine all the ingredients in a bowl, besides the parsley and dill. Whisk the mixture until smooth. Stir in the parsley and dill. Set aside in the fridge until you are ready to serve the salad.

Preheat the oven to 200°C. Cut the cauliflower into florets and combine with the olive oil, spices, and salt and pepper. Roast for 15-20 minutes, or until they have cooked through and are slightly crispy. Leave to cool down.

Blanch the green beans. Bring a pot of water to the boil. Add the green beans and let them cook for about 2 minutes. Strain all the hot water off and run them under cold water until they have cooled down completely. Cut them into thirds.

To assemble the salad, combine the roast cauliflower with the green beans, red onion and rocket on a platter. Just before serving, drizzle over the tahina.

Serves 4-6

Cook's Note
When roasting the cauliflower, make sure the florets are spread out on the baking tray with some space between them so they cook evenly and develop crisp edges. If the dressing is too thick, thin it out with water or lemon juice. You could add toasted nuts or seeds for extra crunch.

Roast Beetroot and Butternut Salad

A beautiful dish that lends colour to any buffet.

- 1 kg beetroot
- extra virgin olive oil
- ½ tsp garlic, crushed
- 1 tsp honey
- salt and freshly ground black pepper
- 1 kg butternut
- 30 g wild rocket
- 180 g Danish feta
- 60 g pecan nuts, toasted and chopped

Cook's Note

Roasting beetroot in foil (rather than boiling) retains both nutrients and flavour. I also prefer the texture.

Cover the beetroot in foil and roast at 180°C for about 30 minutes or until they are cooked through. Once they have cooled down, peel and cut them into batons. Marinate the beetroot with 2 tbsp olive oil, crushed garlic, honey, salt and pepper.

Cut the butternut into wedges, leaving the skin on. Roast them on a baking tray with 2 tbsp olive oil, salt and pepper until golden brown.

To assemble the salad, layer the beetroot, butternut and rocket on a platter. Grate the feta over the salad and sprinkle the pecan nuts over the top.

Serves 10-12

Green Bean, Mangetout and Asparagus Salad
with Sesame and Almonds

- 330 g fine green beans
- 170 g asparagus
- 170 g mangetout
- ¼ cup extra virgin olive oil
- 1 orange, zest
- 1 tsp crushed garlic
- 2 tbsp sesame seeds
- ¼ cup flaked almonds, toasted
- salt and freshly ground black pepper

Cut the green beans in half. Trim the asparagus and cut them in half. Get a pot of water up to the boil. Blanch all of the greens in the boiling water for about 2 minutes until they are cooked through but still crunchy. Strain the hot water off and cool the greens down immediately under running cold water.

Mix the olive oil, orange zest, garlic, sesame seeds and almonds together in a bowl. Add the greens and mix through with salt and pepper.

Serves 6-8

Cook's Note
Blanching correctly is key here. I prefer greens to have some bite, but if you don't, just cook them for longer.

Quinoa and Grilled Vegetable Salad

Quinoa is high in protein and very healthy but quite mild in flavour. I think lemon works particularly well with it and we've added some grated, roasted beetroot to stain it pink.

- 2 medium beetroots
- 2 medium baby marrows
- 1 medium carrot
- 1 medium sweet potato
- 1 red pepper
- 1 yellow pepper
- 1 red onion
- 3 tbsp extra virgin olive oil
- salt and freshly ground black pepper
- 400 g quinoa
- 4 cups water
- 1 lemon, zest and juice

Cover one beetroot with foil and roast in the oven for about 20 minutes or until you can insert a sharp knife into it easily. Once it has cooled down peel the skin off.

Preheat the oven to 180°C. Thinly slice all the rest of the vegetables, including the second beetroot, into equal size pieces. Toss the vegetables with about 3 tbsp olive oil, salt and pepper. Roast them until golden and cooked through. It is best to spread them out onto a large baking tray so that they cook evenly.

In the meantime cook the quinoa in the 4 cups of boiling water for about 8 – 10 minutes or until it has cooked through. Strain the water off and leave it to cool down completely.

Once the quinoa has cooled down, add the lemon zest, juice, and salt and pepper. Grate the roasted whole beetroot and then mix it into the quinoa. Add half the roasted vegetables to the quinoa and toss through gently.

When you are ready to serve the salad, plate the quinoa and then use the rest of roasted vegetables to decorate the salad.

Serves 10 – 12

Barley Salad

- 2 red peppers
- 500 g pearl barley
- ½ cup extra virgin olive oil
- 2 lemons, zest and juice
- 3–4 sprigs oregano, leaves only
- 1 bunch spring onion, finely chopped
- 20 g Italian parsley, chopped
- salt and freshly ground black pepper
- 200 g Kalamata olives
- 200 g Danish feta, cubed
- 30 g basil, leaves only

Cook's Note

Be careful not to overcook the barley – it should still have some bounce. As with any grain, rinse the barley under cold running water before cooking to remove any dirt or grit.

Preheat the oven to 180°C. Roast the peppers for about 30 minutes until slightly blackened. Once removed from the oven, place them into a plastic bag to steam for about 15 minutes. When they have cooled down, remove the seeds and skin and cut them into thin strips.

In the meantime boil the barley in a pot of water for about 15 minutes or until it has cooked through. Be careful not to overcook it. Strain the water off through a colander and leave it to cool down.

Once the barley has cooled down, mix through the olive oil, lemon zest and juice, oregano, spring onion, parsley, salt and pepper. Pit the olives and mix through. Add the peppers and feta. When ready to serve, mix through the basil leaves and plate.

Serves 10–12

Mommy's Lettuce Salad

This is one of my mom's Friday night salads. It is a quick, crisp accompaniment to any meal.

- 350 g crisp lettuce heads
- 120 g pecan nuts, toasted

DRESSING
- ¼ cup canola oil
- 2 tbsp lemon juice
- 2 tbsp white wine vinegar
- ¼ tsp sugar
- ¼ tsp mustard powder
- ¼ tsp paprika
- salt and freshly ground black pepper

For the dressing, combine all the ingredients together and mix well.

Cut the lettuce heads up. Just before serving, dress the lettuce, toss gently and sprinkle over the toasted pecan nuts.

Serves 4

Cook's Note
I prefer toasting nuts in the oven as they brown more evenly and don't burn quite as easily as they do in a pan.

Chickpea and Chopped Vegetable Salad

Take the time to chop the vegetables by hand – this always tastes better than pre-chopped veggies. And for the same reason, don't use tinned chickpeas.

- 400 g dried chickpeas
- 30 g Italian parsley, chopped
- 30 g chives, chopped
- ½ cup black sesame seeds
- ½ cup extra virgin olive oil
- 1 English cucumber, chopped
- 1 red pepper, chopped
- 1 yellow pepper, chopped
- 1 red onion, diced
- 1 lemon, zest and juice
- 1 tbsp za'atar
- salt and freshly ground black pepper

Soak the chickpeas in 3 times the amount of water overnight in a bowl. Strain the water off and wash them under cold running water. Now boil them in a pot of water for about 20 minutes until soft.

Once the chickpeas have cooled down, combine all the rest of the ingredients. Add salt and pepper to taste, and serve.

Serves 10–12

Cook's Note
If you don't like this salad quite so herby and spicy, the quantities can easily be adjusted according to your taste.

Artichoke and Parmesan Salad

I remember eating artichoke leaves as a child in Israel. My safta (grandmother) would dip them in lemon juice, olive oil, salt and pepper – the perfect summer snack. This salad will be at its best if you can find fresh artichokes in season. They are mostly available at fresh produce markets or larger supermarkets.

ARTICHOKES
- 1 tbsp extra virgin olive oil
- ¼ tsp crushed garlic
- ½ red chilli, chopped
- ½ tsp rosemary, chopped
- 100 g fresh artichoke hearts, thinly sliced
- salt and freshly ground black pepper
- 1 tsp lemon juice

DRESSING
- 1 tbsp balsamic vinegar
- 2 tbsp extra virgin olive oil
- 1 tsp honey
- salt and freshly ground black pepper

SALAD
- 100 g rosa tomatoes
- ½ tsp garlic, crushed
- 10 g basil, chopped
- 1 tbsp extra virgin olive oil
- salt and freshly ground black pepper
- 30 g wild rocket
- 30 g baby lettuce leaves
- 30 g Parmesan, shaved
- 20 g pine nuts, toasted

Start by preparing the artichokes. Heat up 1 tbsp olive oil in a pan and fry the garlic, chilli and rosemary for a few seconds. Add the sliced artichokes, salt and pepper, and cook through for a few minutes, stirring every now and then. Turn the heat off and add the lemon juice. Set the artichokes aside to cool down.

Prepare the dressing by mixing the balsamic vinegar with 2 tbsp olive oil, honey, salt and pepper.

In a separate bowl mix together the tomatoes, garlic, basil, 1 tbsp olive oil, salt and pepper. When you are ready to assemble the salad, place the rocket and lettuce leaves onto a platter. Then add the cooked artichokes, marinated tomatoes, shaved Parmesan, pine nuts and dressing.

Serves 4–6

Cook's Note
Out of season, or for less fuss, use bottled artichokes. I often buy these, drain the brine and store in the fridge submerged in extra virgin olive oil, chilli, garlic, lemon, salt and pepper.

Baby Spinach and Nectarine Salad

This salad requires almost no prep and is inspired by my mother-in-law, Jackie.

- 150 g baby spinach
- 3 nectarines, sliced
- 2 avocados
- 100 g peanut brittle, chopped

DRESSING
- 4 tbsp extra virgin olive oil
- 1 orange, juiced
- ½ tsp sugar
- salt and freshly ground black pepper

For the dressing, combine all the ingredients and set aside.

On a platter, assemble the washed spinach with the nectarine slices. Before serving add freshly sliced avocado, drizzle over the dressing and sprinkle over the peanut brittle.

Serves 6-8

Cook's Note
When nectarines are out of season, try substituting grapefruit segments.

Roast Mushroom and Goat's Cheese Salad

- 500 g mushrooms, quartered
- 1 red onion, cut into wedges
- 2 tbsp extra virgin olive oil
- 5 sprigs thyme, chopped
- salt and freshly ground black pepper
- 60 g wild rocket
- 100 g Chevin goat's cheese
- 20 g flaked almonds, toasted
- 30 g pine nuts, toasted

Preheat the oven to 180°C. Combine the mushrooms with the red onion, olive oil, thyme, salt and pepper. Roast the mushrooms on a baking tray for about 20 minutes.

Once the mushrooms have cooled down, mix in the wild rocket, goat's cheese and toasted nuts. Add more olive oil if needed, and be careful not to overmix.

Serves 6

Cook's Note
I've used button mushrooms because they are readily available in supermarkets, but you could use any combination of mushrooms.

Fennel and Radish Salad

This is a new salad at Sababa and a favourite with grilled fish or chicken.

- 150 g fennel bulb, finely sliced
- 20 g red salad onions, chopped
- 40 g radish, sliced
- ½ tsp chilli sauce OR 1 red chilli, finely sliced
- 10 g dill, chopped
- 3 tbsp extra virgin olive oil

DRESSING
- ¼ cup natural yoghurt
- 1 tbsp extra virgin olive oil
- 1 lemon, zest and juice
- 1 tbsp water
- salt and freshly ground black pepper

Combine all the salad ingredients and then combine all the dressing ingredients. When you are ready to serve the salad, add the dressing and mix through. Adjust the seasoning with salt and pepper if needed.

Serves 3-4

Best Roast Potatoes

- 1 ⅕ kg baby Nicola/ Mediterranean potatoes
- ¼ cup extra virgin olive oil
- salt and freshly ground black pepper
- 20 g rosemary sprigs
- 80 g salted butter

Cook's Note

Nicola or Mediterranean potatoes have a waxy texture that works well here. When making these for a dinner party, prepare up to the point where they are about to go into the oven and then allow 40 minutes for finishing before serving. See image on page 92, Preserved Lemon and Chilli Chicken.

Boil the potatoes in a pot of water for about 10-15 minutes until they have just cooked through. Leave them to cool down. Place them onto a baking tray and press them down with your thumb so that they break up slightly. Drizzle over the olive oil and season with salt and pepper. Place a small sprig of rosemary and a small block of butter onto each potato.

40 minutes before serving, preheat the oven to 180°C and roast the potatoes for about 30 minutes or until crispy and golden. These potatoes are best served hot straight out of the oven.

Serves 6-8

Potato Salad with Cream Cheese and Chives

- 1 ⅕ kg Nicola/ Mediterranean potatoes
- 100 ml extra virgin olive oil
- 40 g chives, chopped
- 250 ml cream cheese
- 60 ml cream
- salt and freshly ground black pepper

Boil the potatoes in their skins until they are just cooked through. In the meantime mix together the olive oil, chives, cream cheese, cream, salt and pepper. When the potatoes are ready, cut them into chunks and dress them with the cream cheese mix.

Serves 6-8

Cook's Note
It is important to use Nicola or Mediterranean potatoes as they hold their shape and don't become waterlogged after boiling. The trick is to dress the potatoes while they are still hot so they absorb all the flavours in the dressing.

Fried Cauliflower

This reminds me of a time when I was living in my parents' house and my mom would make fried cauliflower as a side for dinner, just like she did during my childhood. This may not be the healthiest dish, but it is wonderfully comforting – and great as a snack or as part of a mezze spread.

- 600 g cauliflower
- 1 cup flour
- 3 eggs, lightly beaten
- 1 ½ cups breadcrumbs
- ½ cup sesame seeds
- 1 tsp paprika
- 1 tsp cumin, ground
- ½ tsp chilli powder
- salt and freshly ground black pepper
- canola oil for frying

TAHINA SAUCE
- ¼ cup tahini paste
- ¼ cup water
- 1 tbsp lemon juice
- ¼ tsp garlic, crushed
- salt
- 1 tbsp Italian parsley, chopped

You can start by making the tahina dipping sauce. Combine all the ingredients, besides the parsley, using a whisk until smooth. Stir in the chopped parsley. Set aside in the fridge until you ready to serve.

Bring a pot of water to the boil. Place the whole cauliflower into the pot and let it cook for about 2 minutes. Strain all the water off, let it cool down and then cut it into florets.

Place the flour in a bowl, the eggs in another bowl and then have a third bowl with the breadcrumbs, sesame seeds, paprika, cumin, chilli powder, salt and pepper combined.

Add oil to a frying pan so that it is 2 cm high with oil. Once it is hot, you can start to fry the cauliflower. Place the florets into the flour, then into the egg and finally the breadcrumb mix. Then place them into the frying pan and fry until golden and crisp. Keep turning every few minutes so that they cook through all around. Once they are cooked, place them onto a tray with paper towel so that all the excess oil drains off.

Serve while still warm or otherwise heat them up in the oven 10 minutes before serving on 170°C.

Serves 6-8

Watermelon with Feta Salad

There isn't much to it, but I really wanted to share this idea. When visiting Israel during the height of summer, I head down to one of the many beach cafés and order this.

- 400 g watermelon
- 120 g Danish feta
- 10 g basil and mint
- 10 g pine nuts, toasted
- 2 tbsp extra virgin olive oil
- salt and freshly ground black pepper

Cut the watermelon into large chunks and the feta into small slices. Plate the watermelon and feta, and garnish with the leaves of the basil and mint. Sprinkle over the pine nuts and drizzle the salad with olive oil. Season with salt and freshly ground black pepper.

Serves 2-4

Wild Rice with Roast Vegetables and Lentils

Wild rice is not technically rice but a nutritious watergrass seed that is chewy when cooked. I can eat this salad on it's own but it goes really well with chicken and fish.

- 2 cups rice (80% brown rice, 20% wild rice)
- 4 cups water
- 150 g sweet potato, cubed
- 150 g baby marrow, cubed
- 150 g butternut, cubed
- 2 tbsp extra virgin olive oil
- 1 tsp za'atar
- salt and freshly ground black pepper
- 100 g lentils
- 1 lemon, zest and juice
- 20 g mint, chopped
- 10 g Italian parsley, chopped
- ¼ cup extra virgin olive oil

Wash the rice well under running water. Heat 4 cups of water in a pot and cook the rice for about 20-30 minutes until cooked through. The wild rice will still be quite chewy. Strain the water off and leave it to cool down.

In the meantime, roast the sweet potatoes, baby marrow and butternut with 2 tbsp olive oil, za'atar, and salt and pepper on a baking tray for about 25 minutes or until golden and cooked through.

Cook the lentils in boiling water for 10-15 minutes until they are tender but still hold their shape. Strain the water off and leave to cool down.

In a large mixing bowl combine the rice with the lemon zest and juice, mint, parsley, ¼ cup olive oil, salt and pepper. Add half the vegetables and lentils. Plate the rice mix into your serving bowl and then garnish with the rest of the roast vegetables and lentils.

Serves 6-8

RICE DISHES

The following 2 recipes can be used to add texture and flavour to salads and rice.

Spiced Almonds

- 2 cups almond slivers
- 1 tbsp extra virgin olive oil
- ½ tsp salt
- 1 tsp paprika
- 20 g dill, finely chopped

Toast the almonds for about 8 – 10 minutes until golden brown. In the meantime, mix together the olive oil, salt, paprika and dill in a bowl. As soon as the almonds come out the oven, mix them into the bowl with the rest of the ingredients. Leave them to cool before using.

Makes 500 ml

Spiced Seeds

- 1 cup sunflower seeds
- 1 cup pumpkin seeds
- 2 tsp paprika
- 1 red chilli, chopped finely
- 2 tbsp extra virgin olive oil
- 20 g Italian parsley, chopped finely
- ½ tsp salt

Toast the seeds for about 8 minutes until golden brown. In the meantime, mix together the rest of the ingredients in a bowl. As soon as the seeds come out of the oven, mix them into the bowl with the rest of the ingredients. Leave them to cool down before using.

Makes 500 ml

The following 2 methods work best for cooking rice.

Cooking Jasmine Rice

- 1 ½ tsp vegetable oil
- 1 cup jasmine rice
- 1 tsp vegetable or chicken stock powder
- salt and freshly ground black pepper
- 1 ½ cups water

To cook rice the Sababa way, add the oil to the pot in which you're going to cook your rice and heat over a high heat. Add the jasmine rice and cook, stirring, until the rice is toasted. Then add the vegetable or chicken stock (I use Telma), and a pinch of salt and pepper and stir through. Add the water and bring to the boil. Cook over a medium heat with the lid slightly ajar, stirring occasionally, until all the water is absorbed. Lift the lid, lay a clean tea towel over the pot, replace the lid and let it steam for 20 minutes or until you're ready to serve.

Cooking Risotto Rice

Just like the jasmine rice, we cook risotto rice in oil before adding any liquid. This gives a better flavour and good definition to the individual grains.

Wild Mushroom Risotto

This is great as a winter warmer but we also add a parsley-lemon-almond topping, which freshens it up for summer.

- 30 g dried wild mushrooms
- 1 litre water, boiling
- 2 tbsp vegetable stock powder
- 2 onions, sliced
- salt and freshly ground black pepper
- 2 tbsp canola oil
- 1 tbsp crushed garlic
- 500 g button mushrooms, thinly sliced
- 2 sprigs thyme
- 500 g risotto rice
- 2 cups water, boiling
- 50 g salted butter
- 100 g mature cheddar, grated
- 100 g Parmesan, grated

GARNISH
- 1 lemon, zest
- 20 g Italian parsley, chopped
- 30 g almond flakes, toasted

Soak the dried mushrooms in the boiling water with the vegetable stock for about 15 minutes. Fry the onions with salt and freshly ground black pepper in the oil until soft and translucent. Mix in the garlic for a minute or so. Add the mushrooms and thyme and keep cooking until the mushrooms soften and all the liquid has evaporated from the pot. Add the risotto and mix through.

Then add the soaked wild mushrooms and all the liquid. Cook the risotto on a low-medium heat with the lid on for about 15 minutes or until all the liquid has been absorbed. Make sure to stir every few minutes. Add 2 more cups of boiling water and continue cooking on a low heat until all the liquid has been absorbed and the risotto is cooked though. Turn the heat off and add the butter. Once it has melted, mix through the grated cheeses.

Prepare the garnish by mixing the lemon zest, parsley and almonds together in a bowl.

Plate the risotto into bowls and garnish each bowl with a few tablespoons of the parsley mix.

Serves 8 – 10

Green Vegetable Risotto

This is one of our lighter, fresher summer risottos.

- 1 onion, diced
- salt and freshly ground black pepper
- ¼ cup extra virgin olive oil
- 200 g Swiss chard, chopped
- 250 g baby marrow, chopped
- 100 g fine green beans, halved
- 100 g mangetout, sliced
- 2 cups risotto rice
- 3 tbsp vegetable stock powder
- 1 litre water
- 1 broccoli, cut into florets
- 30 g dill, chopped

Fry the onion with salt and pepper in the oil until soft and translucent. Add the Swiss chard and continue cooking until it is soft. Add the baby marrow, green beans, mangetout and mix through. Add the risotto and continue cooking for a few minutes. Mix the stock powder with 1 litre of water and add ¾ of this stock to the pot of risotto.

Cook the risotto on a low-medium heat with the lid on for about 10 minutes and then add the broccoli and dill. If all the liquid has been absorbed and the risotto is not cooked through, add more stock. Continue cooking until all the liquid has been absorbed and the risotto is cooked through, making sure to stir every few minutes. Turn the heat off and leave the risotto to sit for a few minutes in the pot before serving. Check the seasoning and serve with a drizzle of extra virgin olive oil.

Serves 8 – 10

Cook's Note
Try adding some Spiced Almonds or Spiced Seeds (pages 166 – 167) before serving.

Carrot and Onion Rice

- ½ cup canola oil
- 200 g carrots, grated
- 1 ½ cups fried onion flakes
- 4 cups jasmine rice
- salt and freshly ground black pepper
- 2 tbsp vegetable stock powder
- 6 cups water

Heat the oil up in a pot. Add the grated carrots and cook for a few minutes. Add the fried onion flakes and rice. Cook the rice on a medium heat for a few minutes, stirring every now and then. Add salt and pepper and the stock powder and mix through. Add the water, mix through and leave to simmer with the lid on until all the liquid has been absorbed. Turn the heat off and place a clean tea towel over the pot. Press the lid of the pot down and leave the rice to steam for 15 minutes before serving.

Serves 10-12

Sweet Potato and Butternut Risotto with Sage Butter

This is my ideal dish for a lazy Sunday afternoon in colder weather. It is also a hit with dinner-party guests but does require a bit of preparation.

- 400 g butternut, peeled and cubed
- 4 tbsp extra virgin olive oil
- salt and freshly ground black pepper
- 1 onion, chopped
- 1 tsp crushed garlic
- 400 g sweet potato, peeled and cubed
- 2 cups risotto rice
- 1 tbsp vegetable stock powder
- 700 ml water
- 150 g mature cheddar, grated
- 50 g Parmesan, grated

BUTTER SAUCE
- 100 g salted butter
- 10 g sage leaves
- 50 g almonds, flaked

Cook's Note
To prepare the risotto in advance, remove from the heat after the sweet potato has been cooked and allow at least 15 minutes to finish before serving.

Roast the butternut with 1 tbsp olive oil, salt and pepper until soft and golden in colour.

In a pot, fry the onion in the rest of the oil with salt and pepper until soft and translucent. Add the garlic and mix through for a minute. Add the sweet potato cubes and cook for a further minute. Mix through the risotto, stock and 700 ml of water. Place the lid on the pot and simmer for about 10–15 minutes until the risotto has softened and almost cooked through. If all the liquid has been absorbed by the risotto and it is still hard, simply add more water and continue cooking.

Turn off the heat and then mix through the 2 cheeses.

While the risotto is cooking you can prepare the sauce. Melt the butter in a pan on a low heat. Clarify the butter by removing the white foamy topping that settles on the top of the pan once the butter has melted. Continue cooking it on a medium heat until it turns golden. Be careful not to leave it for too long as the butter can burn quickly. Once it is golden, add the sage leaves and fry them until crisp. Remove the pan from the heat and mix through the almonds.

Serve each bowl of risotto with a few tablespoons of the butter and sage sauce.

Serves 6-8

Spanish Rice

I learned this recipe from my mother-in-law, Jackie, and it works well as a base for slow-cooked dishes with complex flavours. I mostly use jasmine rice in my cooking but love using fragrant Basmati rice in this recipe.

- 2 cups Basmati rice
- 2 tbsp canola oil
- ½ tsp salt
- 2 tbsp tomato paste
- 3 cups water

Wash the rice in a sieve under running water. Heat the oil in a pot. Add the rice and mix through. Add the salt and tomato paste and mix through. Add the water, mix through and leave to simmer with the lid on until all the liquid has been absorbed. Turn the heat off and place a clean tea towel over the pot. Press the lid of the pot down and leave the rice to steam for 15 minutes before serving.

Serves 6-8

Herbed Rice

Inspired by a Persian dish, this rice is lovely and herby, fresh and light and great with both fish and meat. That said, we sell lots of this rice at the shop and I often hear people saying they eat it just as it is!

- 4 cups jasmine rice
- ¼ cup canola oil
- 2 tsp salt
- 1 tsp black pepper, ground
- 2 tbsp vegetable stock
- 6 cups water
- 4 cups frozen peas
- 80 g Italian parsley, chopped

Wash the rice in a sieve under cold running water. Heat the oil in a pot. Add the rice and mix through. Add the salt, pepper and stock and mix through. Add the water, mix through and leave to simmer with the lid on until all the liquid has been absorbed. Add the peas and parsley and mix through well. Turn the heat off and place a clean tea towel over the pot. Press the lid of the pot down and leave the rice to steam for 15 minutes before serving.

Serves 10-12

PIES & BAKES

Spanakopitas

I cannot keep up with the demand for these at the shop – we simply do not have the manpower! And they are so light and crisp, you don't realise how many you've actually eaten!

- 2 tbsp extra virgin olive oil
- 1 kg spinach, shredded
- 400 g Danish feta
- 1 egg

PASTRY
- 100 g butter
- 400 g phyllo pastry
- egg for brushing
- sesame seeds

Heat 2 tbsp of olive oil in a pan and cook the spinach in batches until wilted and tender. Leave the spinach to drain off any excess liquid in a colander. Once it has cooled down, make the filling by mixing the spinach, feta and egg together.

Preheat the oven to 170°C. For the pastry, melt the butter in a saucepan. Cut the phyllo sheets into strips about 6 cm wide. Put a heaped tablespoon of the filling near 1 corner of the strip and fold over the phyllo to form a triangle. Brush the rest of the strip generously with butter. Continue folding, maintaining the triangle shape.

Put the triangle seam side down on a baking tray lined with baking paper. Make more triangles in this manner using all the phyllo and filling. Brush the triangles with egg and sprinkle with sesame seeds.

Bake the triangles for about 20 minutes or until golden-brown and crisp.

Makes about 50

Roast Aubergine and Tomato Tart

Our tarts are not to be confused with your usual eggy quiche – we use less egg and more filling.

- 400 g puff pastry
- 150 g baby rosa tomatoes
- extra virgin olive oil
- salt and freshly ground black pepper
- 150 g aubergine, cubed
- 150 g mozzarella
- 80 g Chevin goat's cheese
- 1 egg
- 2 egg yolks
- ½ cup cream
- 2-4 sprigs oregano

Line a 23-25 cm round tart tin with puff pastry and leave it in the fridge to rest. Preheat the oven to 180°C. Roast the tomatoes in 1 tbsp olive oil, salt and pepper on a baking tray until soft. Mix the aubergine cubes with 3-4 tbsp olive oil, salt and pepper and roast on another baking tray until soft and golden. In the meantime, grate the mozzarella and prepare the tart filling by whisking the egg with the yolks, cream and a pinch of salt and pepper.

Once the vegetables have cooled down, fill the tart tin with the roasted aubergine and tomatoes. Add the mozzarella and goat's cheese, and then pour over the tart filling. Garnish the tart with the oregano leaves. Bake for about 30 minutes or until it is a nice golden-brown and the pastry has cooked through.

Serves 6-8

Potato and Caramelised Onion Bourekas

When I was growing up my mother would make these bourekas for special occasions – however, most of them would be eaten before the celebration even began!

- 1 onion, sliced
- 2 tbsp vegetable oil
- salt and freshly ground black pepper
- 500 g potatoes, peeled and cubed

PASTRY
- 600 g puff pastry
- flour
- 1 egg
- sesame seeds for sprinkling

Pan fry the onions in the oil with salt and pepper until soft and brown. Boil the potatoes in water until soft. Strain them through a colander and leave to cool down for a few minutes, allowing all the liquid to strain off. Mash the potatoes until smooth and then mix through the caramelised onion. Check the seasoning and add more salt and pepper if necessary. Set the mixture aside.

Roll out the puff pastry while it is still cold, using a little flour to prevent it from sticking to the surface. Cut the pastry into 5x5 cm squares. Add a spoonful of the filling onto each square and then pinch 2 of the corners together to seal the filling.

Preheat the oven to 170°C. Place all the filled pastries onto a baking tray lined with baking paper. Whisk the egg with a little water and brush each pastry with some egg wash. Sprinkle over the sesame seeds. Bake the bourekas for about 20 minutes or until they are golden, crisp and the pastry has puffed up.

Makes 20

Asparagus Tart with Caramelised Onions and Sesame Seeds

Unlike our other savoury tarts, which take puff pastry, this uses a rich and crumbly shortcrust pastry.

- 1 onion, sliced
- 2 tbsp vegetable oil
- salt and freshly ground black pepper
- 200 g asparagus
- 1 egg
- 2 egg yolks
- ¾ cup cream
- 120 g mozzarella, grated
- 80 g mature cheddar, grated
- 2 tsp sesame seeds

PASTRY
- 250 g flour
- 125 g butter, chopped
- pinch of salt
- 1 egg
- 1–2 tbsp iced water

Cook's Note
Only use fresh asparagus (not tinned) and make it when asparagus is in season.

Start off by preparing the pastry. Sift the flour into a bowl, add the butter and rub it in with your fingertips until the mixture resembles fine breadcrumbs. Stir in a pinch of salt and add the egg and water, and mix to form a firm dough. Knead the dough briefly on a floured surface and then wrap in cling wrap. Leave the dough to chill for at least 20 minutes in the fridge.

Heat the oven to 180°C. Line a 23-cm tart tin with the pastry and then cover it with baking paper and baking beans to weigh it down. Bake the pastry for 15 minutes and then gently remove the paper and beans and cook for another 5 minutes.

Fry the onion slices in the oil with a pinch of salt and pepper until they are soft and golden brown. Trim the asparagus and cut them into thirds. Pour boiling water over them and after a minute strain the hot water off and leave them to cool down. In the meantime prepare the tart filling by whisking the egg with the yolks, cream and a pinch of salt and pepper.

Check the oven temperature (needs to be pre-heated to 170°C). Fill the lined tart tin with the grated cheeses, fried onion and blanched asparagus. Then pour over the egg filling and sprinkle with sesame seeds. Bake the tart for about 30 minutes or until it is golden brown.

Serves 6

Mushroom Pashtida

The Hebrew word pashtida means savoury pie, quiche or casserole, and my mom would often make this pie when having people over for tea. I absolutely love the combination of sautéed mushrooms and caramelised onions.

- 2 onions, sliced
- 3 tbsp vegetable oil
- salt and freshly ground black pepper
- 500 g mushrooms, sliced
- 8 eggs
- 400 g puff pastry, chilled
- extra egg for brushing
- sesame seeds for sprinkling

Cook's Note

You really want to show off the sweetness of the onions, so be sure to cook them until fully caramelised before adding the mushrooms. Cook the mushrooms until all moisture has evaporated and the mixture is completely dry, as any residual liquid will make the pastry soggy.

Fry the onions in oil with salt and pepper until soft and golden. Add the mushrooms and continue cooking until they have browned and all the liquid has cooked away. Lightly whisk the eggs and add to the cooked mushrooms and onions. Keep mixing over a medium heat until the eggs have cooked through. Check the seasoning and add more salt and pepper if needed. Set aside to cool down completely.

Preheat the oven to 180°C. Use a little oil to grease a casserole dish about 20x30 cm. Roll out half the pastry 2–3 mm thick and line the base of the dish with it. Add the mushroom filling. Roll the rest of the pastry 4–5 mm thick and place it on top of the mushroom filling. Now cut the top layer of the pastry into squares of any size. Brush them with egg and sprinkle with sesame seeds. Bake the pie for about 30 minutes or until the pastry is golden-brown and cooked through.

Serves 8

Roast Vegetables and Ricotta Bake

This works as a veggie main or as a side for grilled fish. It is gluten free and the vegetables can be swapped out so it is carb free too.

- 1 medium butternut
- 1 red pepper
- 1 yellow pepper
- 2 medium baby marrows
- 2 medium aubergines
- 1 red onion
- 3 tbsp extra virgin olive oil
- salt and freshly ground black pepper
- 80 g ricotta
- 2-3 sprigs oregano

SAUCE
- ½ onion, chopped
- 2 tbsp canola oil
- ½ tsp garlic, crushed
- 1 chilli, chopped
- 1 tbsp tomato paste
- 500 g ripe plum tomatoes, cut into cubes
- 1 cup water
- 1 tbsp sugar
- salt and freshly ground black pepper

Prepare the sauce by frying the onions in oil until soft and translucent. Add the garlic and chilli and mix through. Add the tomato paste, plum tomatoes, water and sugar. Season with salt and pepper and leave the liquid to come to the boil. Reduce the heat and then leave it to simmer for 20-30 minutes. If the sauce reduces too much, just add a little more water.

Preheat the oven to 180°C. In the meantime, prepare the vegetables by cutting them into equal-sized cubes. Toss them with about 3 tbsp olive oil, salt and pepper. Line a few baking trays with baking paper and roast the vegetables for about 20 minutes or until they have cooked through and are golden in colour.

Once the sauce is made and the vegetables are cooked, combine them in a bowl. Place the mixture into a lasagne dish and crumble the ricotta over. Sprinkle the oregano leaves onto the ricotta. Finish off with some freshly ground black pepper.

Half an hour before you are ready to serve, check the oven temperature or preheat to 180°C. Place the dish into the oven and warm through for about 20 minutes.

Serves 6-8

196

Aubergine Parmigiana

Layered like lasagne but made with aubergines instead of pasta, this Italian
bake is easy to make and the aubergines are meaty and filling.

- 1⁴/₅ kg aubergine, sliced thinly
- ½ cup extra virgin olive oil
- salt and freshly ground black pepper
- 120 g Parmesan, grated

SAUCE
- ½ onion, chopped
- 2 tbsp canola oil
- ½ tsp garlic, crushed
- ½ tsp cumin
- ½ tsp cinnamon
- ½ tsp paprika
- ½ tsp vegetable stock powder
- 2 tbsp tomato paste
- 1 litre tinned chopped tomatoes
- 1 cup water
- 2 tbsp sugar
- salt and freshly ground black pepper

Prepare the tomato sauce by frying the onions in oil until soft and translucent. Add the garlic and mix through and then the spices and vegetable stock powder, letting them cook for a minute. Add the tomato paste, chopped tomatoes, water and sugar. Season with salt and pepper and leave the liquid to come to the boil. Reduce the heat and let the sauce simmer for 20-30 minutes.

In the meantime, prepare the aubergines. Heat the oven to 180°C. Line a few baking trays with baking paper and place the aubergine slices flat onto the baking paper, side by side. Use a pastry brush to brush the aubergine with olive oil. Season with salt and pepper. Roast the aubergines in the oven for about 20 minutes until they are soft and golden.

Once the sauce is made and the aubergines are cooked, you can assemble the aubergine parmigiana. Layer the aubergines with the sauce in a casserole dish, making sure that there is enough sauce for the top layer. Then cover the top layer with grated Parmesan and freshly ground black pepper.

About 45 minutes before you are ready to eat, preheat the oven to 180°C and bake the aubergine parmigiana for about 30 minutes, until the cheese has melted and the top is golden.

Serves 10-12

Spinach, Feta and Parsley Börek

I learned to make this on honeymoon, when my husband Russell and I spent four days on a Turkish gulet. The captain also happened to be the chef, and one morning I watched him make this incredible börek in just a few minutes. Obviously the pastry in Turkey is better suited, but it is still worth making using local phyllo.

- 400 g Swiss chard
- 300 g Danish feta
- 30 g Italian parsley
- ¼ tsp freshly ground black pepper
- 360 g phyllo pastry
- 50 g salted butter, melted
- 3 tbsp extra virgin olive oil

Heat up a large pot, add the Swiss chard and cook just until wilted. Leave it to cool and squeeze out all the liquid. Chop finely and mix together with the feta, parsley and black pepper.

Layer 4 sheets of phyllo pastry at a time with the melted butter. Add a third of the filling along the length of the pastry, leaving a 2 cm border. Brush the rest of the pastry with butter and then roll the pastry up to resemble a long sausage roll. Wet the pastry with some water to soften it slightly. Tuck the one end in, and keep rolling tightly so that the final product looks like a circle. Cover the pastry with a wet tea towel and repeat the process 2 more times.

Heat a large frying pan on a medium heat with 1 tbsp olive oil and fry the pastry one at a time until golden-brown and crisp on both sides. Repeat with the other 2 filled pastries.

This can be made in advance and then reheated for 10 minutes in the oven before serving.

This recipe should make 3 börek rolls.

Serves 4-6

SWEETS & CAKES

Carrot Cupcakes

Although this carrot cake recipe is quite light, it keeps well (without the icing), and I find it is even better after one week – a bit like a Christmas cake!

- 160 g flour
- ½ tsp baking powder
- ½ tsp bicarbonate of soda
- 1 tsp cinnamon
- 1 egg
- 1 egg yolk
- 200 g sunflower oil
- 270 g castor sugar
- 50 g pecan nuts, chopped
- 50 g desiccated coconut
- 120 g carrots, grated
- 1 orange, zested
- 50 g raisins
- 2 egg whites
- pinch of salt

ICING
- 200 g cream cheese
- 80 g unsalted butter
- 40 g icing sugar
- 30 g honey
- 30 g pecan nuts, chopped

Preheat the oven to 170°C. Place 12 large cupcake holders into a muffin tray. Sift the flour, baking powder, bicarbonate of soda and cinnamon together. Lightly whisk the whole egg and egg yolk together. Beat the oil and castor sugar together with an electric cake mixer for about a minute on medium speed. Then on a low speed, slowly add the beaten egg. Mix in the pecan nuts, coconut, carrot, orange zest and raisins, and then add the sifted dry ingredients.

Transfer the mixture into a large bowl. In a clean and dry mixing bowl, whisk the egg whites and salt on high speed to a firm peak. Gently fold the egg whites into the carrot mixture.

Pour the cake mixture into the cupcake holders and bake for about 30 minutes or until a skewer inserted into the centre comes out dry. Leave the cupcakes to cool completely before icing them.

For the icing, beat the cream cheese in a mixer until light and smooth. Remove from the mixer. Beat the butter, icing sugar and honey in the mixer until light and airy. Fold together the cheese and butter mixtures. Spread over the cupcakes and sprinkle with chopped pecan nuts.

Makes about 12

Orange Cake

Sweet honey complements sour oranges in this dense, flourless cake, which can be made up to one week in advance.

- 4 oranges, zested and peeled
- ½ cup marmalade
- ⅓ cup water
- 6 eggs
- 300 g castor sugar
- 1 tsp vanilla essence
- 300 g ground almonds
- 4 tsp cornflour
- 2 tbsp honey
- 2 tbsp water, boiling
- 60 g flaked almonds, toasted
- icing sugar for dusting

Place the peeled oranges, zest, marmalade and water in a saucepan and cook for about 5 minutes on a medium heat. Blitz all the ingredients together using a hand blender so that you are left with a smooth fruit pulp.

Using a cake mixer cream the eggs, sugar and vanilla together until thick and creamy. Once the orange pulp has cooled down, fold it into the egg mixture with the ground almonds and cornflour.

Preheat the oven to 170°C. Line a 23-cm springform tin with baking paper and pour the mixture into the tin. Bake the cake for about 50 minutes or until a skewer inserted into it comes out clean.

Mix the honey with 2 tbsp boiling water and when the cake comes out of the oven, pour over the diluted honey. Leave the cake to cool down and then serve topped with toasted flaked almonds and dusted with icing sugar.

Serves 10

Ricotta Cheesecake

This might be the quickest cake you'll ever make. All the ingredients are mixed in a bowl and then baked in a cake pan, but that doesn't make it any less good! It is much lighter than an American-style cheesecake.

- 900 g ricotta
- 200 g honey
- 5 eggs
- 1 ½ tbsp vanilla essence
- 1 ½ tbsp cornflour
- extra honey and cinnamon
- 6-8 black figs

Cook's Note
We've used figs here, but you can use whatever is available and in season, from berries to dates to nuts or just the honey and cinnamon.

Preheat the oven to 170°C. Whisk the ricotta, honey, eggs, vanilla and cornflour together until the mixture is smooth and there are no lumps. Line a 23-cm springform tin with baking paper and pour the mixture in. Bake the cake until it has just set and still has a slight wobble. Leave it to cool down completely in the tin and then refrigerate.

When the cake is cold, gently remove it from the tin and add a generous amount of honey and cinnamon onto it. Slice the figs and decorate the cake with them. You can drizzle over a little more honey before serving. Keep the cake in the fridge until serving.

Serves 8-10

Nut Ganache Tart

The better the quality of the chocolate, the better this tart will taste.

PASTRY
- 1 egg
- 60 g icing sugar
- 250g cake flour
- ¼ tsp salt
- 180 g unsalted butter, cold and cut into 5-mm dice
- extra flour for rolling

FILLING
- 80 g blanched almonds
- 80 g pecan nuts
- 200 g dark chocolate
- 200 ml cream
- 30 ml brandy
- cocoa powder for dusting

Cook's Note
Use any nuts or, if you prefer, leave them out so it is made only with ganache.

Start by preparing the pastry. Beat the egg and icing sugar together. Put the flour and salt into a food processor and combine for a moment. Distribute the butter over the flour and pulse until just combined. Add the egg mix and pulse again until just combined. Transfer the dough to a lightly floured surface and knead until smooth, taking care not to overwork the dough. Wrap the dough in cling wrap and allow it to rest for an hour in the fridge.

Preheat the oven to 170°C. Remove the pastry from the fridge, allowing it to get to room temperature before rolling out. Line a tart tin with the pastry so that it is about 2 cm thick all around. In this recipe I have used a rectangle tin of 13x35 cm, but you can use any shape tin. Blind-bake the pastry by placing a sheet of baking paper onto the pastry and filling it with dried beans. Bake the pastry for about 15–20 minutes or until it is golden in colour and baked through. Remove the baking paper and beans and bake for a further 5 minutes.

Next prepare the filling. Roast the almonds and pecan nuts in the oven on 170°C for 8 – 10 minutes or until just golden in colour. Leave them to cool down. Chop the chocolate and set aside in a bowl. Heat the cream, making sure it does not boil. Pour the hot cream and brandy over the chocolate and mix them together until smooth.

Add the nuts to the pastry and pour over the chocolate sauce. Let the chocolate settle and then leave it to set in the fridge.

After about an hour, remove from the fridge and gently lift the tart out of the tin. Dust a generous amount of cocoa powder all over and serve at room temperature.

Serves 8–10

Almond and Mixed Berry Slice

A nutty, buttery cake with berries to balance the richness – it is very good served warm with cream on the side.

- 250 g ground almonds
- 250 g icing sugar
- 250 g soft butter
- 4 eggs
- 1 tsp almond essence
- 120 g cake flour
- 180 g cherries
- 100 g blueberries
- 200 g strawberries, halved

Combine the ground almonds and icing sugar. Cream the butter until light and fluffy. Add ⅓ of the almond mixture and mix thoroughly. Add 1 egg and mix until well incorporated. Repeat 2 more times, adding 2 eggs for the last time. Add the almond essence and then fold in the flour.

Preheat the oven to 170°C. Line a deep baking tray, about 20x30x5 cm, with baking paper. Place the mixture in the baking tray. Decorate the cake mixture with the cherries and berries and then bake for about 30–40 minutes or until the cake is golden brown and baked through.

Serves 10–12

Tahini Biscuits

These melt-in-the-mouth biscuits resemble shortbread but have a nutty flavour from the tahini.

- 2 cups flour
- 1 cup sugar
- 2 tsp baking powder
- 300 ml butter, melted
- 1 cup tahini paste
- 2 eggs
- sesame seeds for sprinkling
- castor sugar for dusting

Mix the flour, sugar and baking powder together in a bowl. Add the melted butter and tahini paste and mix through well. Beat the eggs lightly and then add to the mixture to form a dough.

Preheat the oven to 170°C. Roll the dough into balls about 3–5 cm in diameter and flatten them with the back of a fork. Sprinkle over some sesame seeds and bake them for about 10 minutes or until they are golden brown.

Leave them to cool completely in the tray before removing. Dust the biscuits with some castor sugar for extra sweetness.

Makes about 30

Bread-and-Butter Pudding

This pudding is *very* rich, so I've added an apricot compote to serve with it, which I think complements it perfectly.

- 3 cups cream
- ¼ tsp cinnamon
- ½ tsp vanilla essence
- 8 egg yolks
- ½ cup castor sugar
- 7–8 hot cross buns
- 120 g butter, softened
- 120 g apricot jam
- 70 g dark chocolate, chopped
- 40 g raisins

APRICOT COMPOTE
- 200 g Turkish apricots, sliced
- 1 cup water
- ½ cup sugar

CREAM
- 500 ml whipping cream
- 3 tbsp castor sugar

Cook's Note
I've used hot cross buns in this particular recipe, but you can use slices from a good-quality white loaf (not the pre-sliced kind), croissant or brioche.

Prepare the compote by combining all the ingredients in a pot and cooking for 15–20 minutes on a low heat until the apricots have softened and the liquid around them has thickened. Now whisk the cream and castor sugar together until almost stiff. Set aside in the fridge until you ready to serve the dessert.

In another pot heat up 3 cups of cream with the cinnamon and vanilla. Don't let it boil. Whisk the eggs yolks with the castor sugar and then pour the hot cream mixture over. Strain the liquid through a sieve and set aside.

Cut each of the buns into 2–3 thinner slices and spread the butter and jam over generously. In a casserole-type dish about 25x18 cm in size, layer the bread with the chocolate and raisins. Pour over the cream mixture and leave to stand for about half an hour.

About 45 minutes before you are ready to serve the Bread-and-Butter Pudding, preheat the oven to 170°C. Bake the pudding for about 30 minutes or until it turns golden brown and has baked through. Serve it warm together with the cream and apricot compote.

Serves 10

Tiramisu

- 250 g mascarpone
- 250 g cream
- 3 egg yolks
- 100 g castor sugar
- 3 tsp strong coffee powder
- 1 cup water, boiling
- 20 ml rum
- 100 g Boudoir biscuits
- cocoa powder for dusting

Mix the mascarpone and cream together. Using a cake mixer, whisk the egg yolks and castor sugar together until the mixture is pale yellow. When lifting the whisk attachment from the mixture, it should fall slowly forming a ribbon that holds its shape for a few minutes. Fold the thick egg mixture into the cheese mixture.

Mix the coffee, hot water and rum together and leave it to cool. When you are ready to start assembling the dessert, dip the biscuits into the coffee mixture one at a time. Be careful not to leave them in the coffee mixture, or they will fall apart.

Place a layer of biscuits at the base of the dish and then spoon a layer of the cream/cheese mixture over the soaked biscuits. Repeat the whole process until the dish is full. Can also be made in individual dishes. Chill in the fridge before serving and then dust heavily with cocoa powder.

Serves 4–6

Jackie's Greek Shortbread Biscuits

My mother-in-law, Jackie, shared this recipe and I can't believe something so simple can be so delicious. Every oven is different, so you may need to experiment with the temperature to get it right – you don't want these biscuits to brown.

- 250 g margarine
- ¾ cup castor sugar
- ¼ cup sunflower oil
- 1 tsp vanilla essence
- 1 cup ground almonds
- 3 cups flour
- icing sugar for sprinkling

Cook's Note
You could add 1 cup of ground or flaked almonds before adding the flour.

Cream the margarine with the castor sugar until light and fluffy. Add the oil, vanilla, ground almonds and enough flour to form a soft dough (about 3 cups of flour). Be careful not to use too much, you want a rolling consistency.

Preheat the oven to 170°C. Roll into small balls and place on a baking sheet. Press down with a fork. They will spread in the oven so don't place them too close together. Bake for 10–15 minutes. Make sure to watch them as they must not get brown – and remember, every oven is different.

When cool sprinkle with icing sugar.

Makes about 50

Apple and Berry Crumble with Oats and Coconut

I love this recipe for its combination of flavours and textures – you've got the sweet from the apple, the sour from the berries and the soft filling against a crunchy topping.

- 5 large Granny Smith apples, peeled and cubed
- 5 large pears, peeled and cubed
- 1 pinch cinnamon
- 1 pinch nutmeg
- 4 tbsp sugar
- ½ cup water
- 120 g blueberries
- 120 g gooseberries

CRUMBLE TOPPING
- 110 g flour
- 40 g castor sugar
- 1 pinch salt
- 60 g butter
- 50 g coconut flakes
- 50 g pecan nuts, chopped
- 1 pinch cinnamon
- 80 g rolled oats

Cook the apples, pears, cinnamon, nutmeg, sugar and water in a pot for about 10 minutes with the lid on. Continue cooking for a further 10 minutes with the lid off so that most of the liquid is reduced. Turn the heat off and mix the berries through. Leave the mixture to cool down.

In the meantime prepare the topping by crumbling the flour, castor sugar, salt and butter together to resemble breadcrumbs. Mix in the coconut flakes, pecan nuts, cinnamon and oats.

Preheat the oven to 170°C. Place the fruit mixture into a pie dish. Cover with the crumble topping. Bake for 20–30 minutes or until the top is golden brown. Serve the dessert warm with vanilla ice cream.

Serves 10

Lemon Tart

This has a good balance between rich, buttery pastry and tart, lemony filling.

PASTRY
- 1 egg
- 60 g icing sugar
- 250 g flour
- 1 ml salt
- 180 g unsalted butter, cold and cut into 5-mm dice

FILLING
- 8 egg yolks
- 2 tbsp cornflour
- ¼ cup castor sugar
- 2 lemons, zest and juice
- 120 g butter, melted
- ½ cup cream
- icing sugar for dusting
- whipped cream for serving

For the pastry, beat the egg and icing sugar together. Put the flour and salt into a food processor and combine for a moment. Distribute the butter over the flour and pulse until just combined. Add the egg mix to the food processor and pulse again until the dough comes together. Transfer to a lightly floured surface and knead it until it's smooth, taking care not to overwork it. Wrap the dough in cling wrap and allow it to rest for an hour in the fridge.

In the meantime, prepare the filling. Over a double boiler, whisk the egg yolks, cornflour and castor sugar together. Keep whisking until the mixture thickens slightly and lightens in colour. Add the lemon zest and juice, and continue whisking for a few minutes. Remove the bowl from the heat and slowly add in the melted butter, whisking with every addition. Then add the cream and place in the fridge.

Preheat the oven to 170°C. Have a tart tin of 23-25 cm with the removable bottom ready. Now roll out the pastry on a lightly floured surface to about 4 mm in thickness. When the pastry is the desired size, lightly roll it around your rolling pin and then unroll it onto the tart tin. Lightly press the pastry into the bottom and up the sides, getting rid of any excess pastry. Blind-bake the pastry by placing a piece of baking paper over the lined tart tin and covering it with dried beans. Bake the pastry for about 20 minutes or until it is golden brown. Remove the beans and baking paper and pour in the lemon mixture. Continue baking for a further 20 minutes or until the filling has set.

Leave the tart to cool before serving and dust with icing sugar. Serve with fresh whipped cream.

Serves 8-10

Semolina Cake

This traditional Middle-Eastern semolina cake is something my safta (grandmother) on my dad's side would always have in her home for unexpected guests. A strong black coffee or tea counters the extreme sweetness. It will last for a few weeks and should be made at least a day before serving.

- 500 g semolina flour
- ½ cup sugar
- 10 ml baking powder
- 50 g sultanas
- ½ cup ground almonds
- ½ cup orange juice
- ½ cup sunflower oil
- 1 orange, zest
- 1 tsp vanilla essence
- 2 eggs
- 100 g blanched almonds
- extra sunflower oil for greasing

SYRUP
- ½ cup sugar
- ¾ cup water
- ½ lemon, juiced
-

Cook's Note
You could add 2 tablespoons of either orange blossom or rose water to the syrup, or add both and use 1 tablespoon of each. If it is too sweet for your taste, just reduce the amount of syrup.

Combine the semolina flour, sugar, baking powder, sultanas and ground almonds together in a bowl. Add the orange juice, oil, orange zest, vanilla and eggs. Mix everything together well. Don't be alarmed if the mixture seems slightly dry.

Preheat the oven to 180°C. Generously brush oil onto a 20x30 cm rectangle cake tin. Place the semolina mixture into the cake tin and press it down with your hand so that it's compact, level and smooth. Using a sharp knife cut squares 5x5 cm into the cake mix. Place 1 blanched almond into the centre of each square and bake the cake for about 20 minutes or until it is golden brown. If you insert a skewer into the cake, it should come out clean.

While the cake is in the oven, prepare the syrup. Place the sugar and water into a pot and, once it starts to boil, add the lemon juice. Leave it to simmer for about 5 minutes.

As the cake comes out of the oven, pour the syrup over and leave it to cool. Cover the cake squares with cling wrap and serve the following day.

Makes about 30 squares

INDEX

Russell Smith has been shooting professionally for both editorial and commercial clients for over 13 years.

His love for shooting food, together with his wife's love for making it, has culminated in their second book – *Feast with Sababa*.

'What made these two books a pleasure to shoot was that we kept to our disciplines and our strengths.' Russell's intention was to bring his wife's delicious food to life on these pages and make everyone looking at his images want to try to recreate the recipes he knows and loves so well.

First published by Jacana Media (Pty) Ltd in 2016

10 Orange Street
Sunnyside
Auckland Park 2092
South Africa
+2711 628 3200
www.jacana.co.za

© Tal Smith, 2016
Photography © Russell Smith, 2016

All rights reserved.

ISBN 978-1-4314-2408-5

Recipe introductions by Nikki Werner
Cover design by Shawn Paikin
Set in Futura & Garamond
Printed and bound by Imago
Job no. 002806

See a complete list of Jacana titles at
www.jacana.co.za